Historic Tales
of
OLD DUBUQUE

Historic Tales
of
OLD DUBUQUE

JOHN T. PREGLER

THE
History
PRESS

Published by The History Press
Charleston, SC
www.historypress.com

"City of Dubuque." *Drawn and engraved by Charles Vogt; printed by L. Lipman, Milwaukee, circa 1856; author's collection.*

First published 2022

Manufactured in the United States

ISBN 9781467152853

Library of Congress Control Number: 2022939454

This book is dedicated to the memory of my greatest supporter—my beloved mother—Nancy (Hilbert) Pregler.

CONTENTS

FOREWORD

*I*n the following chapters of *Historic Tales of Old Dubuque*, author John T. Pregler has outlined and delved deeply into a number of Dubuque connections to nationally significant people and events. In so doing, he helps the reader understand and appreciate the myriad historical factors that shape the present day and how we all fit into this world. This is the important work of a historian, and by approaching this work from the local lens, John exemplifies why local history is so important.

So often in our primary historical education, we are taught only the main points of key people, dates and events that were significant in our country's timeline. What this leaves out is the very foundation for this sweeping history, and often creates an inaccurate view of the past that lacks nuance and fails to recognize how differently things might have happened. With great attention to detail and meticulous research, John shows the reader how events we may have previously taken for granted as a natural progression were actually the results of small and seemingly insignificant decisions of individuals—the consequences of which echo into the present day. Local history matters because of this. The work of historians like John T. Pregler builds the foundation for our understanding of our collective history and helps make this grandiose history personal, accessible and tangible.

The historical vignettes that follow will surprise the reader and most likely spark curiosity to learn more—they certainly have for me. In the first chapter, the pre-presidential work of Abraham Lincoln shows how closely the history of railroads and politics are intertwined. The following chapter's question about Major Rathbone illustrates the danger of small untruths being repeated, obscuring history in the process. The delicate and precarious situation of the United States during the Civil War becomes increasingly apparent in chapter three's contested election. Frederick Douglass's connection to Dubuque brings this national figure closer to home and offers a glimpse into his personal experiences as he toured the country in the course of his work. In chapter five, the touchstone for this historic event is a water pitcher. As a museum professional, I appreciate that this chapter exemplifies how artifacts connect us to the past and inspire one's curiosity to know more. The final chapter is best summed up in John's own words: "Allison is American history." This chapter shows that Senator Allison is integral to understanding this period of history, with all its promises, successes, errors and failings.

While John has recovered many details previously lost to history, he also recognizes that there is more to uncover. In this, John's understanding of the role of the historian is spot on, and he has illuminated the path for others to follow. His introductory distinctions between relative, collective and personal truths are both timely and necessary. *Historic Tales of Old Dubuque* both educates and entertains, and in it, John proves that there are always more discoveries to be made, untruths to be corrected and details to be uncovered. With his participation in the continual refinement of the historical record, John T. Pregler leads us to a better knowledge of the past, which allows us to more fully understand our present and plan for our future.

—Kristin Glomstad
collections manager and registrar
National Mississippi River Museum and Aquarium, Dubuque County
Historical Society

ACKNOWLEDGEMENTS

There is an extensive list of individuals and organizations who helped in the research, writing and publishing phases required to bring these forgotten stories of Dubuque and American history to print.

I would like to thank my parents, Walter and Nancy Pregler, and my grandmother Olive Hilbert, who fostered my love for history; my proofreader/wife, Cheryl, and my in-laws, Jack and Marge McCarthy; my go-to editor, Tom Barton; historians Clifford Kranik and H. Scott Wolfe; Michael Gibson and the Center for Dubuque History at Loras College; Denette Kellogg and Dubuque's Carnegie-Stout Public Library; Trish Boyer, Kurt Strand and the staff of the National Mississippi River Museum and Aquarium/Dubuque County Historical Society, with a special thank-you to Kristin Glomstad for contributing the foreword to this book; Randy Lyon and EncyclopediaDubuque.org; the Iowa State Historical Society; the University of Dubuque, Charles M. Meyers Library Archives; the Abraham Lincoln Presidential Library and Museum; Chad Rhoad and company at The History Press; and the many more who happily add to history's collective knowledge without their due acknowledgement or a proper thank-you.

I would also like to acknowledge the following organizations for contributing images to this publication and to their dedication to promoting our collective history: the Center for Dubuque History, Loras College; the Collection of John T. Pregler; the Dubuque County Historical Society; the Gilder Lehrman Institute of American History; Heritage Auctions; Hindman Auctions; Leslie Del Toro; the National Portrait Gallery, Smithsonian Institution; the Chicago History Museum; and the U.S. Library of Congress.

Thank you one and all!

INTRODUCTION

If you wou'd not be forgotten
as soon as you are dead and rotten,
either write things worth reading,
or do things worth the writing.
—*Benjamin Franklin,* Poor Richard's Almanac, *1738*

The history of Dubuque and the Tri-State area of Iowa, Illinois and Wisconsin is the history of nineteenth-century America. Dubuque is Iowa's oldest city and one of the oldest settlements along the Upper Mississippi River Valley. From the time Marquette and Joliet first laid eyes on what is now Dubuque, Iowa, in 1673 until the present, Dubuque has been connected to our national history through its people and their deeds of renown or through national figures and their associations to the Tri-State area.

For about a century, just after the end of the Black Hawk War, when the Black Hawk Purchase opened Iowa to settlement, up until the roaring 1920s, Dubuque and the Upper Mississippi River Valley had been a continual beacon of opportunity in the United States, as America's largest natural transportation network, the Mississippi River, crisscrossed with the tracks of the iron horse as railroads and America expanded westward.

Each of the stories contained in this collection reintroduces our contemporary reader to forgotten facts lost to time and history—until now. Each story focuses on events and people and reveals forgotten or unknown portions of history that help fill in or rewrite portions of our collective local and national history.

History, like truth, is multifaceted. Truth has a relative, collective and an absolute side to it, as does history. Relative truth is based on personal experience, understanding and perspective. Collective truths are two or more relative or personal truths brought together, giving a broader perspective of the whole truth related to a person or event in history. Absolute truth is based on all the information for all facets of a topic of truth, or history, under consideration and is in many cases difficult or impossible to obtain.

Relative, collective and absolute truths about our history may and often do seem to conflict with one another, making it the role of the historian to identify, sort out and make sense of all the relative truths and newly discovered information regarding a topic and how they might interconnect. This is especially important, since it is often hard to know the absolute truth when most of our history, written in ages gone by, was written strictly from the singular perspective of the writer. Those who win battles, vanquish peoples or own all the publishing ink tend to write the history and do it from the relative truth they lived, understood or wished to promote. Often, a relative truth may not resemble the relative truth of another participant with a different experience or perspective on the topic. And sometimes, the history we have been told has nothing to do with the truth at all.

The Sioux Nations' truth about Custer's folly at Little Bighorn was never included in the version of history taught or written prior to or during my childhood. Yet, their story and facet of relative truth and history is an extremely critical part of the collective history and absolute truth about Little Bighorn—or, as the Sioux call it, the Battle of Greasy Grass—and our nation's history, and it changes the way we look at the life and times of the people who lived our history in a long ago past.

The role of the historian is also multifaceted. A historian may be a teacher of commonly accepted history, teaching their students how to interpret, critically analyze or question our current understanding of history. A historian may focus on reinterpreting the history of times gone by, giving us a new understanding of historical events or people, as well as our own lives and times and our relationships with one another, all in the hopes of not repeating the mistakes of the past as we look toward a brighter future. A historian may research and write about new information impacting our current understanding of our history, bringing forth forgotten or overlooked people and events in our past that give us a new or better understanding of people, events or a time or place. This can and should force us to change the historical narrative to include or at least consider the new information brought forth by the modern historian.

This book falls in with the latter. For that reason, I have included endnotes with full citations related to the facts behind the stories here presented. I have done so in the hope that other historians—armchair or professional—will critically look at and start including these rediscovered facets in our collective regional and national history in future narratives. I have also included author comments in some of the endnotes.

Frederick Douglass, Abraham Lincoln and Ulysses S. Grant were three of the most influential figures during the second half of the nineteenth century in America. Not only are they three of the most influential Americans of their time, but they are also three of the most well-documented and photographed individuals of the second half of the nineteenth century. Each of these individuals had personal experiences and relationships with individuals in the city of Dubuque that are facets of American history lost to time, only to be rediscovered and presented here as "new" or rediscovered history.

Historic Tales of Old Dubuque includes a crowd of recognizable names from Dubuque and American history. The book finally validates the long-held belief that Abraham Lincoln visited Dubuque in the 1850s and challenges conventional wisdom regarding the congressional service of General William Vandever. In the pages that follow, you will find clarification on open-ended questions in Dubuque history, such as: Did Major Henry Rathbone serve in Dubuque at the start of the American Civil War? And, was an image of Frederick Douglass taken in Dubuque, and if so, when? And finally, learn about a side of U.S. senator William Boyd Allison, once considered the father of the U.S. Senate, that is little known or discussed and how the senator was, in part, responsible for giving us President Theodore Roosevelt.

1

LINCOLN

Riding the Illinois Central to Iowa

PROLOGUE

Legend around Dubuque, Iowa, long held that Abraham Lincoln had visited Iowa's oldest city in the 1850s. Until 2018, no one could say when Lincoln was in Dubuque or what the occasion was that brought him to the western banks of the Mississippi River. Some speculated that Lincoln was in Dubuque in the late 1850s for a weekend respite while trying a legal case in Jo Daviess County Circuit Court in Galena, Illinois. But no one knew this for certain. So, the legend lived on.

Iowa historians had long documented three known instances of Lincoln's visits to Iowa, as well as his other connections to the Hawkeye State. Lincoln is believed to have first stepped on Iowa soil in Davenport in 1857. Lincoln was the attorney for the Rock Island Bridge Company in a famous case between the company and the owner of the steamboat *Effie Afton*, which drifted into the Rock Island Bridge, damaging both the boat and the bridge. Lincoln made a trip to Rock Island, Illinois, to personally inspect the damaged bridge and crossed over the river channel to view the bridge from the Iowa side, marking his first visit to Iowa.[1]

The Illinois rail splitter next visited Iowa on October 9, 1858, giving a rousing political speech at Grimes Hall in Burlington. Lincoln's third and last known visit to Iowa occurred in August 1859, when Mr. and Mrs. Lincoln, along with their travel party, made a special trip from Kansas City to Council

Abraham Lincoln, Chicago, October 1859. *Photographer, S.M. Fasset; Library of Congress.*

Bluffs so that Lincoln could see a piece of land that was put up as collateral in a loan he was associated with. Lincoln also took the time to meet with local Council Bluffs resident and respected railroad engineer Grenville Dodge to get his thoughts on a route and connecting point for a transcontinental railroad.[2]

In January 2018, this author found evidence that Lincoln had indeed visited the Key City to the Northwest. The story of Lincoln's third of four visits into the Heartland is a story about a corporate railroad lawyer and the events of the 1850s that led to his last significant legal case before going on to become president of the United States.

THE LEAD-UP

On Saturday, September 27, 1856, Colonel Roswell B. Mason, engineer-in-chief for the Illinois Central Railroad Company, notified the railroad's board of directors in New York City that its final spike had been driven in, securing the last rail to complete the 705 miles of the longest railroad in the world up to that time. The Illinois Central Railroad Company, or Illinois Central, was chartered by the Illinois General Assembly on February 10, 1851, making it the first of the federal land grant railroads in the United States. On March 22, 1851, the Illinois Central's board of directors chose Colonel R.B. Mason of Bridgeport, Connecticut, as its chief engineer. Construction on the railroad began on Christmas Day, December 25, 1851.[3]

In February 1856, the Honorable Abraham Lincoln, an able circuit court and railroad lawyer from Springfield, Illinois, with political aspirations for himself and his political party, won a crucial victory for the Illinois Central in the state supreme court case *Illinois Central RR v. McLean County, Illinois.* The railroad sued the county, claiming its state railroad charter exempted it from county property taxation because the railroad was already paying a percentage of its revenue to the state. Lincoln spent the rest of 1856 trying to get paid by the Illinois Central for his successful defense of *Illinois Central RR v. McLean County.* That year, he also convinced one of his oldest friends, Jesse Dubois, to join the Republican Party and run for state auditor, while Lincoln set his sights on 1858 and the U.S. Senate seat held by the "Little Giant," Stephen A. Douglas.[4]

Lincoln was a longtime supporter of the Illinois Central and its predecessor, the Cairo City and Canal Company, going back to his early days in the Illinois legislature. He was hired by the organizing company to help lobby for the passage of the state charter in 1851 and worked for the company in one capacity or another until his presidency.[5] Lincoln first represented the railroad as an attorney under legal retainer on April 16, 1853, in the case of *Howser v. Illinois Central Railroad*, which was tried in Bloomington, McLean County, Illinois. Lincoln was hired to defend the railroad when Jonathan Howser appealed an award for property damage caused by the Illinois Central. Lincoln and the railroad lost the appeal.

Railroad engineer Roswell B. Mason, Chicago, 1884. *Photograph by Brisbois; Chicago History Museum.*

Mr. Lincoln's biggest court case for the railroad, although not well known, occurred in two parts in the Illinois Supreme Court in November 1859 and January 1860 in the *People v. Illinois Central Railroad*.[6]

The People v. Illinois Central Railroad

The People v. Illinois Central Railroad was a case that was three years in the making in which Abraham Lincoln was caught between his primary source of income in the 1850s, the Illinois Central Railroad, and a close political ally and warm friend, Illinois state auditor Jesse K. Dubois.[7]

Freshman state auditor Dubois had been threatening to file a lawsuit against the Illinois Central for back taxes that were due even before the Illinois Central paid the first installment on its semiannual tax bill as defined by its state charter, which was first due in October 1857. The state charter under which the Illinois Central operated and was to be taxed was open to interpretation. The state auditor had made it known early on that he interpreted it one way, and the railroad made it known that it interpreted it another way. The state auditor assessed the value of the Illinois Central Railroad using a different assessment method than the one used to value all other railroads operating in the state. Dubois placed the assessed taxable value of the Illinois Central at $19,711,559.59. The Illinois Central's 1857 replacement for Roswell B. Mason, engineer-in-chief and company vice-president, Captain George B. McClellan, believed the railroad was being assessed at four times the rate of any other railroad operating in the state and believed the valuation was more accurately reflected at $4,942,000.00.[8] McClellan and the railroad's board of directors also knew that the Illinois Central was financially in trouble and, with a looming depression and the Panic of 1857 on the horizon, could not afford to pay the state taxes on a property assessment they believed to be inflated and unfair.[9]

In May 1857, Illinois Central president William H. Osborn, in counsel with Illinois Central resident director of the Law Department, Ebenezer Lane, a former justice of the Supreme Court of Ohio, decided to induce Lincoln to use his personal friendship with State Auditor Dubois to help buy the railroad some time with its tax troubles.[10] The Illinois Central had a problem, however. The railroad still had not paid Lincoln for his work from 1853 to 1856 on the case *Illinois Central RR v. McLean County, Illinois*. After nearly a year of trying to collect the fees Lincoln felt were owed to him by the railroad, he filed suit in *Abraham Lincoln v. Illinois Central Railroad* in January 1857.[11]

Mr. Lane had also informed Mr. Osborn that State Auditor Dubois had offered to put Lincoln on the payroll as lead counsel for the state in the impending court battle that would lead to *People v. Illinois Central Railroad*. The state offer was an attractive proposition to Lincoln, as he needed income since he had been fighting his own battle with the railroad for past-due fees. Osborn knew the railroad needed to act quickly to win over the most able lawyer and politician in all of Illinois. Osborn and the railroad worked out a compromise with Lincoln. If Lincoln would reject Dubois's offer and defend the railroad, the railroad would not contest or defend *Abraham Lincoln v. Illinois Central Railroad* and would pay Lincoln his full asking price at the end of the case in a couple of months. Lincoln found the appeal of receiving a much-needed $4,800 desirable and agreed to the Illinois Central's offer.[12]

LINCOLN AND DUBOIS

Jesse K. Dubois and Abraham Lincoln's friendship began in the early days of their political careers in the Illinois House of Representatives, from 1834 to 1842. Both men were active power brokers in the emerging state Republican Party Central Committee in the 1850s.[13] Lincoln first befriended Dubois when they served their freshmen year together in the Illinois state legislature in 1834. Lincoln convinced his old Whig friend to join the Illinois state Republican Party in 1856 and helped get him elected state auditor in that year. That same year, Dubois moved his family to Springfield, just a few doors down from the Lincolns on Eighth Street. The Lincolns and the Duboises would spend countless hours at each other's homes and would even vacation together.[14]

From the moment Dubois took over as state auditor of public accounts on January 12, 1857, he had been publicly scrutinizing the taxable assessment value of the Illinois Central Railroad Company, Illinois's largest corporation, under the provisions of the state's charter.[15] On October 9, 1857, in anticipation of its first semiannual tax payment coming due on October 30, the Illinois Central suspended all payments of debt and was assigned to a three-member trusteeship for financial restructuring. On October 22, Auditor Dubois levied his tax assessment for 1857 against the railroad, with a payment of $86,449.02 due in eight days. October 30 came and passed without a tax payment to the state by the railroad.[16]

On December 21, 1857, Lincoln found himself writing his old friend Dubois on behalf of the Illinois Central Railroad, not as a railroad lawyer to the state auditor, but rather as a lawyer providing his personal opinion to "a friend." Lincoln wrote to Dubois:

> *J.M. Douglas of the ICRR Co. is here and will carry this letter. He says they have a large sum (near $90,000) which they will pay into the treasury now if they have an assurance that they shall not be sued before January 1859—otherwise not. I really wish you would consent to this. Douglas says they cannot pay more, and I believe him. I do not write this as a lawyer seeking an advantage for a client, but only as a friend, urging you to do what I think I would do if I were in your situation.*[17]

John M. Douglas was an old Galena, Illinois, mining lawyer who was then the solicitor for the Illinois Central and one of Lincoln's closest allies and political supporters within the Illinois Central Railroad corporate structure.[18]

Dubois opted to go with the advice of his friend Lincoln and agreed to the proposed terms and received the $86,000 from the Illinois Central into the state treasury. This was a wise move given that the stock market had crashed three months earlier and the Panic of 1857 had begun.[19] The railroad industry and railroad stocks were one of the hardest hit industries during and after the panic started in September 1857, as passenger and freight travel, along with revenues, started to rapidly drop across the country.[20]

1858

Jesse K. Dubois remained relatively quiet about the Illinois Central throughout the majority of 1858. Dubois did this in part due to the December 1857 agreement he made with John M. Douglas and the railroad through Lincoln. Dubois also did it in part to help Abraham Lincoln in his efforts to become the first Republican U.S. senator from the state of Illinois. Lincoln faced off against incumbent U.S. senator Stephen A. Douglas (D-IL) in a series of election debates throughout Illinois in 1858 known as the Lincoln-Douglas debates.

The debates were held in Ottawa, Illinois, on August 21, 1858; Freeport on August 27; Jonesboro on September 15; and then in Charleston on September 18. The debates picked back up in Galesburg, Illinois, on October 7; Quincy on October 13; and the last of the great debates was held in Alton, Illinois, on October 15. The Illinois Central ran special trains from Chicago, Galena, Springfield and other locations to the debate sites.[21] As the debates raged on in Illinois, the nation started to take notice of the Illinois "prairie" lawyer. But not everyone was a fan of Mr. Lincoln.

Illinois Central vice-president George B. McClellan, for one, was a supporter of his fellow Democrat Stephen A. Douglas.[22] Like all the other Illinoisans, Abraham Lincoln and Stephen A. Douglas traveled to and from the debate sites predominately by the Illinois Central Railroad. McClellan offered Senator Douglas the use of his Illinois Central corporate executive car, equipped with a sleeping berth, a dining room and other luxuries not found in common coach. No such offer was made to Mr. Lincoln. Lincoln did have a free pass on the Illinois Central as part of the benefit of being a corporate lawyer on retainer for the company. He did not, however, have access to a private car, for debates or otherwise, as a corporate lawyer for the railroad.[23]

Although Lincoln performed well in his debates against the "Little Giant" and gained favor with the national Republican Party and voters around the nation, he did not come out victorious in the November 1858 election to unseat U.S. senator Stephan A. Douglas. Jesse Dubois had taken notice of the preferential treatment given to Douglas by McClellan and the Illinois Central Railroad during the debates. Dubois also noticed this treatment was not offered in kind to his friend Lincoln—so much so that the day after Stephen A. Douglas was re-elected U.S. senator, Illinois state auditor Jesse K. Dubois filed a legal brief against the Illinois Central Railroad Company in the state supreme court for the back taxes it owed for 1857.[24]

On February 1, 1859, the state supreme court case *People v. Illinois Central Railroad* was officially set to be heard on November 18 of that year in Mount Vernon, Illinois, where the Illinois Supreme Court would be holding session.[25]

PLANNING THE DEFENSE

The railroad turned to Lincoln to lead its defense in *People v. Illinois Central Railroad*. Lincoln and his law partner William Herndon successfully defended the Illinois Central Railroad in a tax case brought by the railroad against McLean County, Illinois, in August 1853.[26] The railroad hoped this time would be no different.

On Tuesday, April 26, 1859, George B. McClellan was in Dubuque, Iowa, staying at the Julien House on railroad business. He departed Dubuque on April 27.[27] McClellan, vice-president and chief engineer of the Illinois Central, was most likely in Dubuque meeting with his predecessor at the Illinois Central and setting the stage for a future visit by railroad officials, including Lincoln.

McClellan, Lincoln and the railroad executives organized a nine-day tour set for July so that state officials could inspect every mile of railroad track and all the properties owned by the Illinois Central Railroad in a process of discovery in the case *People v. Illinois Central Railroad*. The railroad hoped that it and the state would come to a mutually agreeable valuation more in line with the railroad's estimates for the 1859 tax year. It was decided that Lincoln, as corporate lawyer and lead counsel for the case, would lead the tour. Lincoln would bring along Illinois Central's board of director member and company trustee John Moore. The trip was promoted as the state auditor's assessment tour of the Illinois Central, which was his legal duty under the state charter. The *Freeport Weekly Journal* headline declared, "On an Inspecting Tour—State Auditor."[28] The *Chicago Tribune* headline read, "Assessment of the Illinois Central Road," and its report pointed out the "duty of the auditor of public accounts to annually assess for taxation the Illinois Central Railroad."[29]

The railroad decided to make the trip a bit more enjoyable for the travel party by allowing everyone to bring their families. To ensure the party was able to effectively conduct railroad business, the board of directors provided a private locomotive with a private car, presumably the executive car McClellan had allowed Senator Douglas to use during the Lincoln-Douglas debates just ten months prior.[30]

The assembled travel party consisted of railroad executives, state officials and appraisal experts, with almost everyone having a close connection to Lincoln. On the trip were Jesse K. Dubois, state auditor; Ozias M. Hatch, secretary of state; William H. Butler, state treasurer; former state lieutenant governor John Moore, an Illinois Central board member; Thomas H. Campbell, former state auditor; and, in a role originally offered to Lincoln, Judge Stephen T. Logan, special counsel for the state. Jesse Dubois, Stephen Logan and Thomas Campbell brought their wives with them on the trip. Mary Todd Lincoln joined her husband on the trip, along with the Lincoln's two youngest sons, William, or Willie, and Thomas, or Tad, Lincoln.[31]

From the outside, the trip appeared to be more of a vacation among old friends than a state railroad business venture, and Abraham Lincoln was the common denominator. Lincoln had known William Butler since his early days in New Salem and had lived with Butler and his family for over five years. He first met Dubois in the state legislature in 1834. Ozias Hatch and Lincoln had worked closely as political comrades in Illinois state politics. Lincoln was a frequent visitor to Hatch's office in Springfield when Hatch was secretary of state and would take Hatch's personal clerk, John G. Nicolay, to Washington, D.C., to be his personal secretary in the White House. Butler, Dubois, Hatch and Lincoln, along with Illinois Civil War governor Richard Yates, were the real powerbrokers of Illinois Republican politics during its infancy. Judge Stephen T. Logan, who was on the trip as special counsel to the state auditor, was once Lincoln's law partner in Springfield, from 1842 to 1844, and had known and worked with Lincoln before and after their partnership. Mary Todd Lincoln was especially fond of Mr. Hatch and Mrs. Dubois.[32]

TRAVELING THE ILLINOIS CENTRAL

On Thursday, July 14, 1859, the travel party, including the future president and his family, boarded the private train provided for the trip and departed Springfield, Illinois, to assess the lines and property of the Illinois Central Railroad.[33] In 1859, the Illinois Central Railroad started at the southern tip of Illinois in Cairo and ran north through Jonesboro and Carbondale and into Centralia, Illinois, east of St. Louis. In Centralia, the Illinois Central split into two lines, with the Chicago Line running to the northeast and into Chicago. The Galena, or Main Line, ran north through the prairies of Decatur, Bloomington, La Salle and into Dixon. From Dixon, the line contoured the rolling hills all the way to Freeport. From Freeport, the line cut through the deep valleys and the high bluffs around Galena and into the northern terminus of the Illinois Central Railroad in the river town of Dunleith, Illinois, across the Mississippi River from Dubuque, Iowa.[34] (Dunleith is the present-day city of East Dubuque, Illinois.)

The party set out from Springfield to Decatur along the Western Railroad. In Decatur, they merged onto the Illinois Central Railroad lines and headed north for Dunleith in the northwestern part of the state. The party could only travel thirteen hours a day, all during daylight hours, so the lines and railroad property could be observed and assessed. This trip was especially brutal, as daytime temperatures ranged from 98 to 108 degrees around Illinois and Iowa that week.[35] Based on Illinois Central Railroad timetables, the party would require approximately sixteen hours of travel time from Springfield to Dunleith, broken up over two days to accommodate for daylight travel, with frequent stops to assess properties and load up on fuel and water for the locomotive.

On Saturday, July 16, the Lincolns' private train rolled into Freeport, Illinois, for a stop. The *Freeport Weekly Journal* stated on July 21, "Dubois, Sec. Hatch, Ex-Gov. Moore, 'Old Abe' and several other gentlemen from Springfield passed through this city on Saturday last on a special train bound for Dunleith....They stopped over here for several hours and were shown 'the lions' by some of our citizens."[36] After departing Freeport, the party would have stopped in Galena to assess the Illinois Central station and properties there. From Galena, it was on to the northernmost terminus of the Illinois Central in Dunleith.

It is not hard to imagine Lincoln telling Willie and Tad stories of his days as a captain in the Black Hawk War as the locomotive rolled through the rock cuts and high bluffs of northwestern Illinois between Freeport and Galena. Maybe he told them about the day in 1856 that he gave a speech to a large crowd in the streets from the second-floor balcony of Galena's DeSoto House, or maybe he even told them stories of the Meskwaki village at Dubuque's lead mines, when Natives and wild beasts still roamed the prairies of Illinois and Iowa.

Upon reaching the railroad station in Dunleith on Saturday, July 16, the travel party prepared for a stopover in nearby Dubuque, Iowa.[37] Lincoln, along with Mary, his children and the rest of the travel party, disembarked from the train at the station at the end of Sinsinawa Avenue in Dunleith. Grabbing some of their personal belongings for their stay in Dubuque, the party started to make their way toward the Mississippi River to cross over

The *Dubuque Herald* announcing that the "Hon. Abram Lincoln" is staying at the Julien House, July 19, 1859. *Author's collection.*

into Dubuque. In 1859, the closest railroad bridge that crossed the Mississippi River from Illinois to Iowa was between Rock Island, Illinois, and Davenport, Iowa. Travelers and cargo transported on the Illinois Central Railroad to and from Dubuque through the Dunleith terminal had to cross the Mississippi River at Dubuque by river ferry until January 1869, when the Dunleith and Dubuque Railroad Bridge opened. The Lincoln party was no exception. Like all other travelers and cargo, the thirteen-member Lincoln party traveled the one thousand feet from the Illinois Central station to the Dubuque and Dunleith Ferry landing on the eastern banks of the Mississippi River, across from the Dubuque Harbor and Jones Street on the western banks of the Mississippi River.

Lincoln had history with the Dubuque and Dunleith Ferry going back to its beginning. In 1837, territory pioneer George Wallace Jones petitioned the Illinois state legislature for a charter to operate a ferryboat between Dunleith, Illinois, and Dubuque, which was then part of the Wisconsin Territory. Upon the recommendation of a mutual friend in Springfield, Jones enlisted the aid of a young state legislator by the name of Lincoln to introduce legislation granting Jones the charter. Lincoln was successful in getting the legislation passed.[38]

After crossing the river on the Dubuque and Dunleith Ferry, the party, having secured a ride on the Iowa side, headed west on Jones Street, turning north onto Main Street and traveling three blocks to the Julien House, Dubuque's premier hotel. Unlike he did on many of the trips he was making between 1856 and 1860, Lincoln did not make a public or political appearance while in Dubuque. It is unknown what the party did while in Dubuque. Whether Mary Todd Lincoln and her two boys were out and about Dubuque to explore the rapidly growing Key City to the Northwest or took in a show at one of Dubuque's theaters, we do not know.

A young Dubuque railroad lawyer and Iowa Republican by the name of William Boyd Allison heard that the great Illinois Republican from the Lincoln-Douglas debates was in town. Most likely, Allison and others had learned of Mr. Lincoln's arrival by the conspicuous presence of a private locomotive and coach parked in Dunleith and the news—and rumors—that spread with its arrival. Allison wished to see Lincoln in the flesh, so he, along

Above: Julien House, Second and Main Streets, Dubuque, circa 1870. *Center for Dubuque History, Loras College.*

Right: William Boyd Allison, U.S. representative, 1865. *Photographer, Matthew Brady; Library of Congress.*

with some other enthusiastic young Republicans, including his law partner George Crane, went to the Julien House to see if they could catch a glimpse of the great debater, who was then only seven months away from giving his linchpin speech at Cooper Union in New York City that would launch him directly into the White House. Allison would later say, "When I heard he was in town, I went to the hotel to see him. However, I didn't feel important enough to make his acquaintance."[39]

The Dubuque and Pacific Railroad

Living in Dubuque at the time of Abraham Lincoln's visit in July 1859 was none other than Colonel Roswell B. Mason, George B. McClellan's predecessor as engineer-in-chief of the Illinois Central Railroad. Mason had moved to Dubuque in 1856, after completing the Illinois Central, in order to start constructing the Dubuque and Pacific Railroad, which traveled from Dubuque to Dyersville, Iowa.[40] Mason had signed on as the Dubuque and Pacific Railroad's chief engineer from its beginning on April 28, 1853, while he was still engineer-in-chief and superintendent of the Illinois Central Railroad.[41] Mason, along with Illinois Central president Robert L. Schuyler, were original members of the group of individuals who first organized and incorporated the Dubuque and Pacific Railroad.

Led by Lucius H. Langworthy, an original founder of the City of Dubuque in 1833, the Dubuque and Pacific Railroad was formally incorporated on May 19, 1853. Langworthy was joined by Mason and Schuyler, along with Jesse P. Farley, the railroad's first president; Platt Smith, the railroad's attorney; Frederick S. Jesup, the railroad's treasurer and brother of Morris Ketchum Jesup, a prominent New York banker and railroad financier; Judge John J. Dyer; F.V. Goodrich; Robert Walker; Robert C. Waples; Edward Stimson; Captain G.R. West; Dr. Asa Horr; Mordecai Mobley, a Dubuque banker, early settler of Sangamon County, Illinois, and friend of Abraham Lincoln; and United States senator George Wallace Jones (D-IA), the railroad's first chairman of the board.[42]

George Wallace Jones, while serving a term as the U.S. congressional delegate for the Wisconsin Territory in 1838, was the first person in Congress to propose appropriating federal funds to build a transcontinental railroad, connecting the Atlantic Ocean with the Pacific Ocean. The idea was based on the request, research and planning done by Jones's Dubuque constituent, John Plumbe Jr.[43] Plumbe, a civil engineer, helped

Left: U.S. senator George W. Jones, 1859. *Right*: U.S. senator Stephan A. Douglas, 1859.
Photographer, Julian Vannerson; Library of Congress.

finance his national campaign to build a transcontinental railroad with profits from his wildly successful chain of Plumbe's National Daguerrian Galleries and the sale of photographic equipment he manufactured. Plumbe died in 1857, never seeing his dream of a railroad from sea to shining sea realized. Plumbe was buried in Dubuque's Linwood Cemetery and is considered by many to be the father of American photography and the transcontinental railroad.

Jones next played a critical part in U.S. railroad history when, as a U.S. senator from Iowa, he was successful in amending Senator Stephan A. Douglas's Federal Land Grant Act of 1850, which provided federal land to the state of Illinois for the creation of the Illinois Central Railroad. Jones's amendment extended the proposed terminus of the Illinois Central from Galena, Illinois, to Dubuque, Iowa, by way of Dunleith, Illinois.[44] The successful passage of Jones's amendment upset the citizens of Galena and created friction between Senator Douglas and the people of Galena in the 1858 U.S. Senate race. During the Senate race between Lincoln and Douglas, Douglas accused his fellow senator George Wallace Jones of underhanded politics in getting the terminus of the Illinois Central extended from Galena to Dubuque in 1850. Jones, a Democrat, took offense to the accusations and came out in support of Douglas's opponent, Republican Abraham Lincoln, for the U.S. Senate seat in 1858.[45]

ROSWELL B. MASON

The Dubuque and Pacific Railroad was conceived as a natural extension of the Illinois Central Railroad, connecting the eastern and western sides of the Mississippi River and allowing the Illinois Central to extend its presence into Iowa and on to the Pacific Ocean. This would also connect the Dubuque and Pacific to the markets of the east coast and the Atlantic Ocean. The plans also called for a railroad bridge to be built across the Mississippi River at Dubuque, connecting the Dubuque and Pacific directly to the Illinois Central. The bridge came close to becoming a reality on February 14, 1857, when the Illinois state legislature approved a charter for the Dunleith and Dubuque Bridge Company.[46] And engineer Roswell B. Mason was to be the architect of it all. The construction of a railroad bridge was delayed by more than a decade due to the Panic of 1857, the depression that followed and the events of the American Civil War.

Mason moved to Dubuque after resigning as chief engineer from the Illinois Central and the Dubuque and Pacific Railroad in 1856. Mason, along with his partner Ferris Bishop, started Mason, Bishop and Co. in Dubuque,

A check to Mason, Bishop and Co. for the construction of the Dubuque and Pacific Railroad, November 1857. It was signed by J.P. Farley, the namesake of Farley, Iowa. *Author's collection.*

a railroad construction company, which, in turn, was hired by the Dubuque and Pacific Railroad to prepare the route, build the bridges and lay the tracks for the railroad from Dubuque to Dyersville, Iowa. Mason, Bishop and Co. was located in the same building as the Dubuque and Pacific Railroad, the Julien Theater building at the northwest corner of Fifth and Locust Streets.[47] Replacing Mason as chief engineer of the Dubuque and Pacific Railroad in 1856 was one of his associate engineers who was responsible for building the Illinois Central from Eldina, Illinois, near La Salle, to Dubuque—Benjamin B. Provoost.[48]

It is highly likely Lincoln and John Moore, along with state officials, met with Colonel Mason and Benjamin Provoost during their visit to Dubuque. There is a strong possibility the meeting was preplanned during George B. McClellan's visit to Dubuque less than three months prior. Mason's office was only four blocks from where the Lincoln party was staying in Dubuque, and it would not have been the first time Lincoln and Mason had met—nor would it be the last. Both men had worked at the pleasure of the board of directors of the Illinois Central Railroad since the early 1850s.

Colonel Mason was a key witness called by Lincoln in his landmark case *Hurd v. Rock Island Bridge Company* in 1857. The case revolved around Jacob S. Hurd and his steamboat, the *Effie Afton*. Hurd had struck two bridge piers as he tried to navigate the *Effie Afton* past the first railroad bridge built across the Mississippi River between Rock Island, Illinois, and Davenport, Iowa. The boat was destroyed, and the bridge was damaged by the incident. Hurd claimed in his lawsuit that the bridge presented an obstruction to the free navigation of the Mississippi River, and therefore, the bridge company was responsible for the damages to his steamboat. The Rock Island Bridge Company hired Lincoln to defend it. Lincoln enlisted the aid of an eminent railroad engineer living in Dubuque, Roswell B. Mason, to help build the defense. Mason testified over the course of two days in the case and described his experience building railroad bridges in the East and throughout Illinois. Mason described a series of tests and experiments he conducted with floats to evaluate the flow and current of the river in relation to the placement of the bridge piers at Rock Island. He related these experiments to piloting a steamboat, navigating the river currents, and the ability for railroad bridges and steamboats to successfully coexist in the Mississippi River through intelligent engineering design.[49] It was this testimony that helped Lincoln win this case, which was critical to railroads across the nation.

Roswell B. Mason would also go on to be one of three key witnesses that Lincoln called to testify in the Illinois Supreme Court case *People v. Illinois Central Railroad* in November 1859.[50] This is the case that led the Lincoln travel party to assess all the lines and properties of the railroad, and it led Lincoln to Dubuque.

LINCOLN DEPARTS

Lincoln and his travel party left Dubuque and Dunleith on the morning of Monday, July 18.[51] Just four years prior, on July 18, 1855, U.S. senators George Wallace Jones (D-IA) and Stephan A. Douglas (D-IL) were in Dunleith to dedicate the grand opening of the Illinois Central line from Eldena to Dunleith and the arrival of the first train a few weeks earlier.[52]

The travel party arrived in Chicago later that evening. The *Chicago Tribune* noted in its "Personal" section that the party checked into the Tremont House, located at the southeast corner of Lake and Dearborn Streets in downtown Chicago. After spending Tuesday, July 19, in Chicago, the party left for Cairo, Illinois, at the southern tip of the state.[53] The Lincoln travel party finally arrived back in Springfield late on Friday, July 22, successfully wrapping up a nine-day, 705-mile tour of the properties of the Illinois Central Railroad.[54]

EPILOGUE

Abraham Lincoln would go on to successfully defend the Illinois Central Railroad Co. in the case *People v. Illinois Central Railroad*, appearing before the court in Mount Vernon, Illinois, on November 18 and 19, 1859, to address the railroad's assessment value for the 1859 tax year. Lincoln appeared before the court again on January 12, 1860, to address the outstanding issue of back taxes due for 1857 and 1858. Lincoln's three key witnesses in the case were Illinois Central vice-president George B. McClellan, former Illinois Central chief engineer Roswell B. Mason and the then-current railroad chief engineer of the Illinois Central, Leverett H. Clarke. The high court handed down its decision on the company's assessment valuation on November 21, 1859, finding in favor of Mr. Lincoln and the Illinois Central Railroad.[55] The court handed down its decision on the company's back taxes for 1857 and 1858 in February 1860, again finding in favor of Lincoln and the railroad.[56]

Old acquaintances meet. President Lincoln and General McClellan in Antietam, Maryland, October 3, 1862. *Photographer, Alexander Gardner; Library of Congress.*

Abraham Lincoln would give his Cooper Union speech in New York City seven months after his visit to Dubuque, Iowa. From there, he would go on to beat Stephan A. Douglas in the 1860 presidential election, becoming the sixteenth president of the United States on March 4, 1861.

George B. McClellan would go on to become President Lincoln's commanding general of the U.S. Army on November 1, 1861, at the beginning of the American Civil War. President Lincoln relieved General McClellan of his command on November 5, 1862, for not pursuing Confederate general Robert E. Lee after the Union's victory at the Battle of Antietam. McClellan would go on to lose to President Lincoln in the 1864 presidential election as his Democratic challenger.

Jesse K. Dubois, Ozias M. Hatch and William H. Butler worked selflessly to get their friend Lincoln elected president in 1860. They each remained active in Illinois Republican politics and continued to communicate with their longtime friend and comrade President Lincoln on state and national political matters. Jesse Dubois would eventually become cynical about a lack of personal political favors from President Lincoln but would always remain loyal to Lincoln the man and his memory. Dubois would play a key role in bringing the martyred president back to Springfield, Illinois, in 1865 and seeing him buried on behalf of his grieving friend Mary Todd Lincoln, who was too crippled by grief to participate.

Ozias Hatch was with President Lincoln in October 1862 and accompanied him on a visit to the Antietam Battlefield to see General McClellan. It was to Ozias Hatch during this visit that Lincoln famously referred to the Army of the Potomac as "General McClellan's bodyguard." Mr. and Mrs. Jesse Dubois and Ozias Hatch joined Mr. and Mrs. Lincoln when they visited Council Bluffs, Iowa, in August 1859, one month after their visit to Dubuque.[57]

U.S. senator George Wallace Jones (D-IA) would unburden himself of his interest in the Dubuque and Pacific Railroad under the company's restructure that occurred after the Panic of 1857. The Dubuque and Pacific reorganized as the Dubuque and Sioux City Railroad in 1860, which ultimately became the property and primary line through Iowa for the Illinois Central Railroad. Jones would also sell some of his riverfront property in Dunleith to the Illinois Central Railroad for the construction of a railroad bridge between Dunleith and Dubuque. Jones received lifetime passes on the Illinois Central Railroad for himself and his family as part of his compensation for the land. The Dubuque lawyers representing the Illinois Central in the land sale were none other than George Crane and U.S. representative William Boyd Allison (R-IA).

Representative Allison was elected to the U.S. Congress in 1862 and developed a working relationship with President Lincoln during his administration. Allison was also the president of the Dunleith and Dubuque Bridge Company. Both Jones and Allison met with President Lincoln on separate occasions in the White House during the Lincoln administration.[58]

The chief engineer Allison selected to oversee the construction of the Dunleith and Dubuque Railroad Bridge in 1867 was none other than Roswell B. Mason, the builder of the Illinois Central and Dubuque and Pacific Railroads and Lincoln's star witness in two of his most important railroad cases as a corporate lawyer. Mason served as the original chief engineer for the Illinois Central Railroad Company, the Dubuque and Pacific Railroad Company and the Dunleith & Dubuque Bridge Company. He also served as Superintendent of the Illinois Central and President of the Dubuque and Pacific Railroad at one time or another. With the completion and opening of the Dunleith and Dubuque Railroad Bridge in 1869, Mason resigned from the company and returned to Chicago.[59]

The Dunleith and Dubuque Railroad Bridge under construction by Andrew Carnegie's Keystone Bridge Company, 1868. *Photographer, Samuel Root; author's collection.*

Roswell B. Mason was elected mayor of Chicago in November 1869. Mayor Mason was at the end of his term when legend says Mrs. O'Leary's cow kicked over a lantern and started the Great Chicago Fire on October 8, 1871. Mayor Mason sent telegraphs to his friends in nearby cities, including the city of Dubuque, requesting immediate assistance of any kind. Calls went out to Dubuque, Milwaukee, Detroit and other Midwest communities. City of Dubuque officials immediately provided Mayor Mason with $2,500 in cash from the city's treasury, and the citizens of Dubuque sent food, clothing and other necessities over the next couple of months.[60]

All of the Dubuque donations to the victims of the Great Chicago Fire were delivered over the railroad bridge and tracks Roswell B. Mason personally built over the prior two decades of his life, the same railroad tracks that brought an influential railroad lawyer named Abraham Lincoln to Dubuque, Iowa, in July 1859.

2

MAJOR RATHBONE ON DUTY IN DUBUQUE

*W*ith the explosive crack of the assassin's Derringer pistol, Major Henry Rathbone jumped to his feet in an effort to detain J. Wilkes Booth in the presidential box at Ford's Theater. Booth, in his struggle to get away, pulled out his dagger and stabbed Major Rathbone in his right arm before jumping over the balcony railing and onto the theater stage below, yelling and waving his dagger wildly as he made his escape into the night. Through the actions of a deranged madman on April 14, 1865, Major Henry Rathbone was thrust into the spotlight of American history.

Certainly, Henry Rathbone had thought by April 9, 1865, the day Confederate general Robert E. Lee surrendered to Union general Ulysses S. Grant at Appomattox Courthouse in Virginia, he would survive the war. This was a major achievement, given that Henry Reed Rathbone was a fighting member of the Twelfth U.S. Infantry, a regiment that had seen heavy action in twelve eastern battles, including the Battles of Gaines' Mill, Antietam, Fredericksburg, Gettysburg and Weldon Railroad, and had suffered significant casualties as a member of the Army of the Potomac during the war.[61] And now the major, wounded and bleeding, tried frantically to get the barricaded door open to the presidential suite as the president of the United States lay dying.

President Lincoln would die of his mortal wound a few hours later, on April 15, 1865. Major Rathbone would be treated for his non-life-threatening wound and would begin to answer the questions all Americans were asking, like who was Major Henry Rathbone? And what happened in President Lincoln's suite at Ford's Theater?

Left: Major Henry Rathbone accompanied President and Mrs. Lincoln to Ford's Theater. *Photographer, Mathew Brady, 1865; from Wikimedia Commons.*

Right: Lincoln assassin J. Wilkes Booth, as he was known. *Photographer, Alexander Gardner, circa 1865; Library of Congress.*

RATHBONE IN DUBUQUE

Word of President Abraham Lincoln's assassination spread across the nation like wildfire and first appeared in the *Dubuque Democratic Herald* newspaper on April 16. Articles about the assassination, those involved in the dastardly deed and the chase, capture and execution of the conspirators would dominate American newspapers for several months. The American public wanted to know more about those who were targeted and injured that fateful evening. Local communities around the United States, in both the North and South, reflected on their connections to the figures and events that played out on the national stage. Dubuque, Iowa, was no different. The *Dubuque Democratic Herald* ran a two-sentence article on page one of its April 18 edition titled "Major Rathbone":

> *Some people think that the Major Rathbone who was in the private box with the president the night he was killed and who was himself wounded was the Captain Rathbone who was on duty in Dubuque during the first*

*year or two of war. We have not yet seen his initials and therefore cannot
state, but there is a large family of Rathbones in Albany, and several of
them are engaged in the war, so that it cannot be positively asserted that it
is the same one.*[62]

Henry Reed Rathbone of Albany, New York, was a major in the Twelfth
U.S. Volunteer Infantry that originated from Fort Hamilton in New York
Harbor. Upon joining the Twelfth U.S. Infantry in May 1861, Captain Henry
Rathbone was immediately assigned to recruiting services and remained on
recruiting duty until March 1862.[63]

The Twelfth U.S. Infantry had recruiting offices in different cities across
the northern part of the United States at the start of the Civil War, including
an official recruiting office in Dubuque, Iowa.[64]

Dubuque Recruiting

The city of Dubuque was teeming with recruiting offices during the first two
years of the Civil War, 1861 and 1862. Dubuque was a natural rendezvous
point for men from northern Iowa, Wisconsin, Minnesota and northern
Illinois seeking adventure in the army because the city was connected to
two vital transportation networks. Dubuque, Iowa, was one of the largest
cities along the Mississippi River between St. Louis, Missouri, and St. Paul,
Minnesota, and it was located at a major intersection for steamboats and the
railroads of the northwest.

Recruiting offices sprang up around Dubuque starting in April 1861 to
raise men to answer President Lincoln's call for soldiers to put down the
rebellion of the South. Camp Union was built at Eagle Point to drill, quarter
and muster into military service the men who were pouring into the city to
join one of the Iowa regiments that were being organized in Dubuque by
order of Iowa governor Samuel Kirkwood.

In 1861, Dubuque's Camp Union was the regimental headquarters and
mustering center for the Ninth and Twelfth Iowa Infantries and the Third
Iowa Light Artillery. Recruiting offices were established in the city of
Dubuque and companies were also raised for the First, Third and Seventh
Iowa Infantry; the First Iowa Light Artillery; and the First, Fifth and Seventh
Iowa Cavalry, all of which had regimental headquarters in other Iowa cities.[65]

In 1862, Dubuque's Camp Franklin, renamed from Camp Union, was the
regimental headquarters and mustering center for the Twenty-First, Twenty-

A check to Major Carl Schaeffer, signed by Captain (Edward) C. Washington, 1861. Both men were killed during the Civil War. *Author's collection.*

Seventh, Thirty-Second and Thirty-Eighth Iowa Infantry. Recruiting offices were established in the city of Dubuque and companies were raised for the Sixteenth, Thirty-Seventh, Forty-Second, Forty-Fourth and Forty-Sixth Iowa Infantry, all of which had regimental headquarters in other Iowa cities.[66]

Recruiting offices were also set up in Dubuque for out-of-state regiments and for U.S. Volunteer Infantry regiments. The Eleventh Pennsylvania Cavalry raised Company A in Dubuque. The Third Missouri and the Twenty-Ninth Illinois Infantry also raised companies in Dubuque. The federal army recruited men through Dubuque as well. The Twelfth, Thirteenth, Sixteenth and Nineteenth U.S. Infantries all had recruiters and recruiting offices operating in Dubuque in the first couple of years of the war.[67]

The Thirteenth U.S. Volunteer Infantry was highly successful while recruiting in Dubuque and raised several hundred soldiers through its Dubuque office. The Thirteenth U.S. Infantry was organized in 1861, with William Tecumseh Sherman as its colonel and Philip Sheridan as one of its senior captains. Captain Edward C. Washington and Lieutenant John M. Duffy were recruiting officers for the Thirteenth U.S. Infantry in Dubuque. Captain Washington would also perform the honors of mustering into service numerous Iowa regiments and/or companies that were being organized and mustered into service at Dubuque's Camp Union in 1861 and Camp Franklin in 1862.[68] Captain Washington died on May 2, 1863, from wounds he received previously in the Battle of Chickasaw Bayou, near Vicksburg, Mississippi.[69]

TWELFTH U.S. INFANTRY

The Twelfth U.S. Infantry was organized by decree of President Lincoln on May 4, 1861. The regiment was organized at Fort Hamilton in New York Harbor. William B. Franklin of Pennsylvania was the regiment's organizing colonel.[70]

Henry Reed Rathbone joined the Twelfth U.S. Infantry with his Union College Class of 1857 classmate Samuel S. Newbury of Detroit, Michigan, on May 14, 1861. Captain Rathbone and First Lieutenant Newbury began their service in the Twelfth as regimental recruiting officers. They joined fellow Union College alumnus Daniel Butterfield, class of 1849, who was the Twelfth U.S. Infantry's organizing lieutenant colonel.[71] Butterfield would go on to create the enduring military bugle call "Butterfield's Lullaby," known today as Taps, in 1862.[72]

After the organization of the officer's corps for the Twelfth U.S. Infantry, it was decided that recruitment would be handled by sending the regimental captains, along with their lieutenants, to their home states to recruit men for companies they would then lead. The regimental captains were from New York, Pennsylvania and Ohio, as well as Indiana, Illinois and Minnesota.[73]

First Lieutenant Newbury was paired with Captain Thomas M. Anderson of Ohio. Captain Anderson was the nephew of Major Robert Anderson of Fort Sumter fame. It was decided by the regimental command that Captain Anderson would recruit in his home state of Ohio, and Lieutenant Newbury, who was listed as being from Detroit, would be assigned to recruit in Wisconsin in the northwest.[74]

The Twelfth U.S. Infantry ultimately chose Dubuque, Iowa, as the location of its recruiting office in the northwest. First Lieutenant Samuel Newbury was the officer in charge of the recruiting office, located at Main and Third Streets in Dubuque.[75] Although Newbury was not listed as being from Dubuque, it was a homecoming of sorts for the young lieutenant. Newbury's father, Reverend Samuel Newbury, had moved his family to Dubuque nearly a decade earlier. Reverend Newbury was a Presbyterian minister and missionary from Vermont who ministered throughout the United States. Newbury moved to Dubuque in 1853.[76] Mary Newbury Adams, the minister's daughter and the young lieutenant's sister, was married to the prominent Dubuque attorney Austin Adams.[77]

Second Lieutenant W.W. Dewey from Fort Hamilton was in Dubuque recruiting alongside First Lieutenant Newbury. The Twelfth U.S. Infantry mustered over two hundred soldiers from Dubuque into service between

1861 and 1862.[78] This was a large number of soldiers, and the majority of them were recruited by a local enlisted soldier, Private James Jackson, who had moved to Dubuque in the 1850s. Jackson would quickly rise through the ranks and spend a career in military service, eventually retiring from the U.S. Army as a lieutenant colonel with a Congressional Medal of Honor for the courage he displayed in risking his life to retrieve the body of a fallen comrade in a battle against the Nez Perce in 1877.[79]

Samuel Newbury's connections to Dubuque extended even further to his time at Union College. Rathbone and Newbury were members of the class of 1857 at Union College in Schenectady, New York. Joining them at Union College were fellow classmates Franc Wilkie of West Charleston, New York (class of 1857), and Alexander Simplot of Dubuque, Iowa (class of 1858). Both Wilkie and Simplot were living in Dubuque at the start of the Civil War in 1861 and were part of the news corps "Bohemian Brigade" that followed General Grant's army around the western theater of the war in 1861 and 1862. They reported on the war through the written word of Wilkie in the *Dubuque Herald* and the *New York Times* and the sketches of Simplot in *Harper's Weekly Journal*.[80]

There are six degrees of separation between Lincoln's assassination, Henry Rathbone and Dubuque: (1) Lincoln's assassination and witness Henry Rathbone; (2) Rathbone recruiting for the Twelfth U.S. Infantry; (3) Rathbone's connections with Dubuque-connected alumni from Union College; (4) Rathbone and his friendship with Samuel Newbury; (5) Newbury and the Twelfth U.S. Infantry's Dubuque recruiting office; and (6) the *Dubuque Democratic Herald*'s article. They all collectively connect like pieces of a puzzle to show that Rathbone was in Dubuque at the start of the war. The question the *Dubuque Democratic Herald* posed on April 18, 1865, regarding whether Captain Henry Rathbone was in Dubuque recruiting soldiers in 1861 or 1862, however, is not as evident as the pieces may originally suggest.

In May 1863, the Twelfth U.S. Infantry was down to four recruiting offices. While its headquarters was located with the regiment in the field, the Twelfth had recruiting offices at Fort Hamilton in New York Harbor; in Elmira, New York; and in Philadelphia, Pennsylvania. The Twelfth's fourth recruiting office was the Dubuque, Iowa office that had been in operation since 1861.[81]

Once a regiment was staffed and in the field, especially a battle-hardened regiment like the Twelfth U.S. Infantry, a steady flow of new recruits was needed to replenish the ranks. Between death from disease, accidents and battle, and losing individuals who were wounded, sick, captured or made a prisoner of war or who either deserted or left at end of their enlistment, regiments were continuously in need of soldiers and therefore recruited new men throughout the war.

A RATHBONE ON DUTY IN DUBUQUE?

So, the question posed by the *Dubuque Democratic Herald* on April 18, 1865, would suggest that it is possible Captain Henry Rathbone of the Twelfth U.S. Infantry was in Dubuque in 1861 and/or 1862, helping recruit for the Twelfth U.S. Infantry. But is it probable? The prior empirical connections mentioned support the possibility and even lend support to the probability that Henry Rathbone spent the first year or two of the Civil War in Dubuque. But by no means is it definitive.

Rathbone's military records are short on specifics and do not give any indication that he was either in Dubuque or would have been prevented from being in Dubuque in 1861 or early 1862. The records are vague regarding where he served while on recruiting duty, but they do clearly state that Henry Rathbone joined the Twelfth U.S. Infantry on May 14, 1861, and served as a recruiting officer from that May until March 1862.[82] This period falls within the period the *Dubuque Democratic Herald* suggested Rathbone might have been in the Key City, as well as the timeframe we know his classmate Samuel Newbury was active in Dubuque, recruiting for the Twelfth U.S. Infantry.

A May 1863 article in the *Philadelphia Inquirer* titled "The Regular Recruiting Service" discussed the status and location of each of the nineteen regular U.S. Army infantry units, their headquarters, the location of their recruiting offices and the names of their recruiting officers. The Twelfth U.S. Infantry listed a total of nine recruiting officers located at Fort Hamilton in New York Harbor; in Elmira, New York; in Philadelphia, Pennsylvania; and in Dubuque, Iowa. Fort Hamilton had six recruiting officers assigned to it. Elmira, Philadelphia and Dubuque each had one recruiting officer assigned to them in May 1863. Dubuque's recruiting officer was listed as Captain Rathbone—Captain Joel H. Rathbone.[83]

THE RATHBONES

Joel H. Rathbone joined the Twelfth U.S. Infantry in February 1862, after resigning from the U.S. Navy in January that same year. Joel Rathbone had served in the navy since October 1858. His first and last assignment in the Twelfth U.S. Infantry was as a recruiting officer. It is not clear when Captain Rathbone was first assigned to the recruiting office in Dubuque, but it is clear he served in Dubuque until he took command of one of the companies in the Twelfth U.S. Infantry in June 1863, when he joined his nephew Henry Rathbone in the field just in time for the Battle of Gettysburg in July 1863.[84] Joel Rathbone was the much younger brother of Henry Rathbone's father, Jared Rathbone.[85]

It is unclear if Joel Rathbone was sent to Dubuque to replace Samuel Newbury as a recruiting officer or if the two served together while recruiting in Dubuque. Letters between Samuel Newbury's sisters Mary Adams and Frances Bagley of Detroit from 1861 and 1862 suggest that sometime between October and November 1861, Samuel Newbury arrived in Dubuque. The letters also suggest Newbury had "assistants"—plural—helping him recruit, which was not uncommon. The sisters' correspondence show that Samuel Newbury was still in Dubuque on April 27, 1862.[86] It is likely Newbury left Dubuque to join the Twelfth U.S. Infantry in the field when he received his promotion to captain on July 21, 1862.[87] It is also likely Joel Rathbone was assigned to the Dubuque recruiting office shortly after joining the regiment in 1862, serving in Dubuque until June 1863.[88]

Does this mean the Captain Rathbone the *Dubuque Democratic Herald* was referring to was Joel Rathbone, Henry Rathbone's uncle? Or could both Rathbones have served in Dubuque? It is clear Joel Rathbone was at least one Rathbone from Albany who served in Dubuque in 1862–63. The *Herald* article, however, suggested that its Rathbone served in Dubuque in 1861–62. Is it possible both Henry and Joel Rathbone spent time in Dubuque recruiting for the Twelfth U.S. Infantry? It seems possible, although seemingly less probable.

EXAMINING THE POSSIBILITY

The *Dubuque Democratic Herald* stated, "Some people think that the Major Rathbone who was in the private box with the president the night he was killed and who was himself wounded was the Captain Rathbone who was on duty in Dubuque during the first year or two of war." There are two clues in this wording that may—or may not—suggest the article is referring to Henry Rathbone. The first clue is in the first three words of the article: "some people think."

If "some people think" the Rathbone who was with President Lincoln that fateful night was the same Rathbone who served in Dubuque, it would stand to reason that these people had an occasion or cause to believe, or "think," it was the same Rathbone of the Twelfth U.S. Infantry who was recruiting in Dubuque "the first year or two of war." Which brings us to our second clue: "the first year or two of war."

Does this second clue suggest that the Rathbone in question was in Dubuque the first year of the war—and possibly the second year, too? Or is it suggesting that the Rathbone in question was in Dubuque during either the first year of the war or the second year of the war? Regardless, Joel Rathbone was on duty in Dubuque sometime between March and June 1862 until June 1863, during the second and third years of the war.

It is possible that both Captain Henry Rathbone and his uncle Captain Joel Rathbone were in Dubuque recruiting for the Twelfth U.S. Infantry at different times during the Civil War. It is also possible the *Herald*'s article was referring to Henry Rathbone based on the people who knew him and knew if and when he was in Dubuque. Perhaps Dubuque residents Mary Newbury Adams and her husband, Austin Adams, were "some people" who questioned whether the Major Rathbone who was in Ford's Theater was the same Rathbone who served in Dubuque with Mary's brother Samuel, a college classmate of Henry Rathbone. If Rathbone was in Dubuque when Newbury was there, he could have been introduced to Mary and Austin Adams by Samuel. And that could be why "some people think" it was Captain Henry Rathbone who was on duty in Dubuque and also in the president's box. Samuel Newbury never got to speak about his relationship with his comrade who accompanied Mr. and Mrs. Lincoln to Ford's Theater that fateful night in 1865. Captain Newbury was killed while trying to surrender to Confederates at Weldon Railroad, near Petersburg, Virginia, on August 19, 1864. He was buried in Linwood Cemetery in Dubuque.[89]

It does not appear that the *Dubuque Democratic Herald* ever followed up on its April 18 article on Major Rathbone to answer the question posed. Perhaps this was because Henry Rathbone was not on duty in Dubuque at the beginning of the war. The only Rathbone who appeared in the military record who was connected with recruiting for the Twelfth U.S. Infantry in Dubuque, Iowa, was Captain Joel Rathbone. Although this does not rule out that Henry Rathbone also recruited in Dubuque at the beginning of the war, it does make it much less likely.

3

WILLIAM VANDEVER

Iowa's Congressman-Colonel

On February 10, 1863, Special Order No. 41 was issued from Major General Ulysses S. Grant's headquarters of the Department of the Tennessee, stationed in Youngs Point, Louisiana. The special order granted a twenty-day furlough to Brigadier General William Vandever, U.S. Volunteers, giving him "permission to proceed beyond the circuits of [the] department."[90]

General Vandever was heading to Washington, D.C., to participate in the last days of the closing session of the Thirty-Seventh U.S. Congress, for which Vandever was reelected to the House of Representatives from the Second Congressional District of Iowa on October 9, 1860. Representative Vandever (R-IA) was headed to the capital to defend his honor, which had been called into question in the national newspapers and on the floor of Congress. Vandever had been at the center of a yearlong congressional debate resulting from a resolution from the House Committee on Elections, which declared that Representative Vandever was not entitled to his seat in Congress from the time he was mustered into the service of the United States in Dubuque as colonel of the Ninth Iowa Infantry on September 24, 1861.[91]

LeGrand Byington of Iowa City, Iowa, was traveling around the state of Iowa and Washington, D.C., making claims that Vandever had not been legally elected to the seat in 1860 and that he, LeGrand Byington, was the only person in Iowa, since Vandever's military commission, to receive votes in the October 1861 election to replace Vandever.[92] Byington was also accusing Vandever of double-dipping into the U.S. Treasury, receiving taxpayer-backed pay as both a congressman and as a military officer of the United States.[93]

An appeal to Representative Samuel S. Cox (D-OH) to contest Representative Vandever's seat on the floor of the House of Representatives was made in writing on November 27, 1861, by Byington. Byington claimed he was elected to succeed Vandever. Byington's nine-point appeal was read on the floor by Cox and referred to the House Committee on Elections on December 2, 1861.[94]

Two questions were raised by Byington's appeal to the House. First, was Byington duly elected by the citizens of Iowa to replace Vandever, and should he be allowed to take the seat in the U.S. House of Representatives? The second question was more important because it would impact at least eighteen members of Congress and perhaps the balance of

General William Vandever, U.S. Volunteers, circa 1865. Photo by Alex. Hesler. *Heritage Auctions.*

power.[95] The second question raised by Byington's appeal was whether a member of Congress could simultaneously serve in the U.S. military as the American Civil War was moving into full swing in 1861. At the outbreak of war, numerous members of the U.S. Congress, like Vandever's peer, Iowa representative Samuel Curtis, resigned their seats in Congress to take command of regiments in their home states.

Some, like Colonel Vandever, did not resign their seats. Most observers argued that the U.S. Constitution addressed this matter in section 6 of article I regarding the legislative branch and representatives' compensation. The second paragraph of section 6 states:

> *No senator or representative shall, during the time for which he was elected, be appointed to any civil office under the authority of the United States which shall have been created, or the emoluments whereof shall have been increased during such time; and no person holding any office under the United States, shall be a member of either House during his continuance in office.*

William Vandever was first elected to the U.S. Congress as a representative for Iowa's Second District in 1858. Vandever, a member of the Iowa

Republican Party since 1856, served two terms as Iowa's representative in Congress from March 4, 1859, until March 3, 1863. Vandever served in the Thirty-Sixth and Thirty-Seventh U.S. Congress, leaving office with the expiration of his second term on March 3, 1863, while he was simultaneously serving as brigadier general in Major General Grant's Army of the Tennessee.[96]

Representative Vandever's official congressional biography states he "served from March 4, 1859, to September 24, 1861, when he was mustered into the Union army as colonel of the Ninth Regiment, Iowa Volunteer Infantry, never having resigned his seat in Congress." This and other sources suggest Vandever abandoned his seat in Congress without resigning or returning to the House chambers after September 1861.[97] History tells us otherwise.

BEFORE THE WAR

William Vandever was born in Francis Scott Key's Baltimore, Maryland, on March 31, 1817. After receiving a general education in Maryland and Pennsylvania, Vandever moved to the Mississippi River town of Rock Island, Illinois, in 1839, seeking to stake out his future in the northwest frontier country, where just seven years earlier, Black Hawk and his band of Sauk Natives lost their bid to do the same. After holding several jobs, including a stint as a land surveyor for the U.S. surveyor general, Vandever moved one hundred miles up the Mississippi River to Dubuque, Iowa, in 1851 to study law under railroad attorney Platt Smith. He was admitted to the Iowa bar in 1852.[98]

Vandever developed his Dubuque law practice over the next six years, first partnering with a young, up-and-coming lawyer and want-to-be politician, Democrat Benjamin M. Samuels, in 1853 and 1854.[99] Samuels moved to Dubuque in 1848 to practice law. He was elected Dubuque city attorney shortly after arriving in Dubuque. Active in the Democratic Party, Samuels was elected to the state legislature in 1854 and nominated for governor in 1857, losing to Ralph P. Lowe.[100]

By 1857, Vandever was partnered in the Dubuque law firm Vandever, Friend and Shiras. Junior law partner George Shiras Jr. would go on to serve on the U.S. Supreme Court from 1892 to 1903. Shiras left the firm and the city of Dubuque in 1858 at the same time William Vandever found himself running to succeed one-term congressman Timothy Davis of Dubuque

U.S. Representative William Vandever, circa 1860. *Photographer, Mathew Brady; Library of Congress.*

for the Second Iowa Congressional District seat in the U.S. House of Representatives. Davis and Samuel Curtis were the first two Republicans elected to the U.S. House of Representatives from Iowa.

Vandever surprised the state by beating his Democratic challenger William Leffingwell and joining the Thirty-Sixth U.S. Congress in March of 1859.[101] Vandever won reelection to his seat in the election of 1860, when he found himself running against his former Dubuque law partner, Benjamin M. Samuels.[102]

Secession

With the election of Abraham Lincoln to the presidency in November 1860 came the secession of states, starting with South Carolina in December 1860. Congressman Vandever immediately went to work suppressing secession and preserving the Union. On January 3, 1861, Vandever represented Iowa on the Border State Committee. The committee contained one congressional member from each of the border states of Kentucky, Maryland, Ohio, New Jersey, Delaware, North Carolina, Tennessee, Indiana, Virginia, Illinois, Missouri, Arkansas, Iowa and Pennsylvania and made a failed effort to prevent any of the fourteen states from seceding and to find a resolution to the conflict facing the nation in the hour of its greatest need.[103]

On January 25, Vandever offered a joint resolution in the House of Representatives on his position on the question of secession, stating that no grounds existed for the dissolution of the Union and that southern states found secession—and the possibility of war—more expedient than amending the Constitution. Challenging his northern brethren to resist giving into the will of the secessionists, Vandever pointed out "a government which cannot execute its own laws is not fit to be maintained."[104]

Vandever was also a member of the failed Peace Conference held at Washington's Willard Hotel in February 1861 in a final effort by northern and southern politicians and civic and religious leaders to avert an all-out civil war. The conference debated four competing proposals, including the Crittenden Compromise and the Border State Proposition. The last two plans, according to Vandever, would have enshrined the perpetual protection of slavery into the U.S. Constitution, which, he declared, could not be allowed.[105]

The Peace Conference failed to produce a proposal that was acceptable to both the North and the South. Both sides immediately began preparing for the coming storm. The South continued organizing and building its new federal government, the Confederate States of America (CSA), and seizing United State government property and military installations throughout the South, with an eye on Fort Sumter in South Carolina's Charleston Harbor. In the North, the U.S. Congress continued to struggle with how to deal with the seceding states as President Buchanan sat idly by and the nation nervously prepared for the new presidential administration of Abraham Lincoln. While serving as a member of the Peace Conference, Vandever also served on the Presidential Inauguration Ball Committee for the incoming president.[106]

After the firing on Fort Sumter on April 12, 1861, just a little over a month after President Lincoln's inauguration, the U.S. Congress went into full swing preparing for war. Men, from both the North and South, started to gather and form large armies. In the North, congressmen left the U.S. Congress to raise and lead soldiers, while others helped their state governors organize and raise the regiments called for by President Lincoln. Congressman Vandever, working with Iowa governor Samuel Kirkwood, wrote in the newspapers of Iowa on April 22, calling for volunteers. Vandever pleaded, "Men of Iowa, rally! God and your country call!"[107]

On June 18, 1861, Congressman Vandever was entertaining thoughts of leading an Iowa regiment like his former congressional counterpart from Iowa's First District Colonel Samuel Curtis. Writing to Charles Aldrich, a Republican newspaper editor in Webster City in northern Iowa, Vandever said he is waiting on authority to raise his own regiment, and if received, the Counties of Wright, Hamilton, Webster, and Hardin would have a chance of raising companies and joining the regiment and the war.[108]

Four days before the first famous battle of the Civil War along Bull Run Creek near Manassas, Virginia, Congressman Vandever, along with Senator Henry Lane (R-IN) and Representatives Schuyler Colfax (R-IN), John Verree (R-PA), Elihu Washburne (R-IL), August Frank (R-NY), John Pettit (R-IN) and Albert Porter (R-IN) traveled with an advance guard of General Irwin McDowell's Union army to Fairfax, Virginia, twenty miles outside of Washington, D.C., to inspect the buildup of federal and Confederate troops.[109] Four days later, on July 21, 1861, Vandever was one of the many members of Congress and citizens of Washington who traveled the thirty-five miles to Manassas to witness parts of the First Battle of Bull Run.[110]

The next day on the floor of the House of Representatives, Vandever offered a resolution, proclaiming:

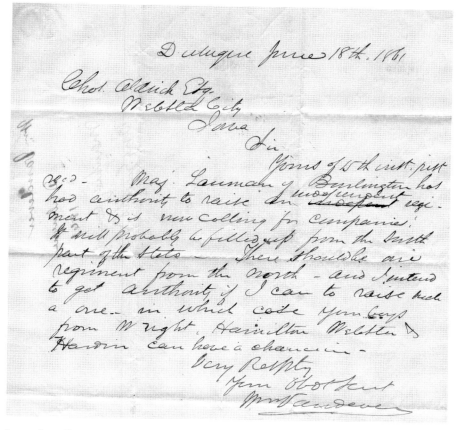

Letter from Representative Vandever to Iowa newspaper editor Charles Aldrich, informing him of his intention to raise a regiment, June 18, 1861. *Author's collection.*

Resolved, that the maintenance of the Constitution, the preservation of the Union, and the enforcements of the laws, are sacred trusts which must be executed; that no disaster shall discourage us from the most ample performance of this high duty; and that we pledge to the country and the world the employment of every resource, national and individual, for the suppression, overthrow, and punishment of rebels in arms.

Vandever's resolution, which, in essence, committed the U.S. government to the position that individual states are not permitted to secede from the perpetual union of the federation, passed with unanimous consent.[111] Averting a civil war was not to become reality, and President Lincoln was forced to call for seventy-five thousand volunteers to squash the rebellion.

CONGRESSMAN TURNED COLONEL

Congressman William Vandever received permission to raise and lead the regiment he wrote to Charles Aldrich in Webster City about—the Ninth Iowa Volunteer Infantry. On September 12, 1861, the *Madison State Journal*, reporting on affairs in Dubuque, noted that the Ninth Iowa Infantry was being raised under "Colonel and Congressman Vandever," indicating that it was known Vandever had not resigned his seat in Congress before raising his regiment.[112] On September 24, 1861, Congressman William Vandever was formally mustered into military service as the colonel of the Ninth Iowa Infantry, and he left Dubuque for St. Louis with his regiment the next day.[113]

Vandever and the Ninth Iowa spent October and November 1861 guarding railroads around Franklin, Missouri. With the monotonous life that comes with the army's winter downtime, Colonel Vandever left the Department of the Missouri in Rolla at the beginning of December and joined his brother congressmen in the U.S. House of Representatives for the second session of the Thirty-Seventh U.S. Congress.[114]

Back in Iowa in October 1861, the *New York Herald* reported, "A man named LeGrand Byington set himself up for Congress in the Second District of Iowa at the recent election and received about one thousand votes. He first declared the seat of Hon. Wm. Vandever vacant, because he took the field in defence [*sic*] of the Union and then announced himself as a candidate."[115]

Byington, an Iowa Democrat who was opposed to the war and the Lincoln administration, saw a potential opportunity to secure Vandever's seat in Congress based on article I, section 6 of the U.S. Constitution. Article I prohibits an individual from holding two offices within the U.S. government simultaneously. Byington, of his own volition and without official authority, declared Vandever's seat vacated and got his name placed on numerous county ballots for Vandever's Iowa Second District congressional seat. This was done even though Vandever did not resign his seat, the State of Iowa did not declare a special election, the Iowa Democratic Party did not nominate Byington and the next official election was not slated to take place until October 1862. Byington, the only name on the ballot for the seat, received roughly one thousand votes and declared himself the winner. The State of Iowa did not recognize or certify the election.[116]

LeGrand Byington could not be in Washington, D.C., for the start of the second session of the Thirty-Seventh Congress to contest Colonel Vandever's seat in the hopes that Congress would expel their brother representative and turn the seat over to Byington. Byington was a radical

Copperhead Democrat and former Ohio state legislator in the vein of Representative Clement Vallandigham (D-OH), the leader of the northern antiwar Democrats during the Lincoln administration.[117] Byington wrote to Vallandigham's fellow Ohio Copperhead member of the House Samuel S. Cox, asking him to read a "memorial" on the floor of the House of Representatives that he had prepared.[118] Representative Cox presented Byington's nine-point memorial on December 2, 1861, and it was referred to the House Committee on Elections as *LeGrand Byington vs. William Vandever* and ordered to be printed for the public.[119]

Colonel Vandever was in the Union capital during the second session and was residing at the Washington House along with several other members of Congress, including Vice President Hannibal Hamlin.[120] The colonel cast his first vote in the session on December 4, 1861, on HR7, a resolution securing homesteads to settlers, and he would cast nearly two dozen votes between December 4, 1861, and January 10, 1862, before returning to his military post.[121] This was after September 24, 1861, the date that Vandever's official congressional biography states he was no longer a U.S. representative.

While in the capital city, the congressman-colonel learned of the orders that were given for his Ninth Iowa Infantry to march on the enemy. Vandever departed Washington, D.C., by train posthaste for the unit's camp near Rolla, Missouri, arriving in late January.[122] Colonel Vandever and the Ninth Iowa, part of the Second Brigade of the Fourth Division of the Army of Southwest Missouri, marched through southern Missouri and into northwestern Arkansas in pursuit of Confederate general Sterling Price.[123]

In early March, two large armies led by Confederate major general Earl Van Dorn and Union brigadier general Samuel Curtis met near Elkhorn Tavern, a quiet trading post and inn northeast of Fayetteville, Arkansas, in the Battle of Pea Ridge. Colonel Vandever, Major Francis J. Herron and their Ninth Iowa Infantry distinguished themselves before and during the critical battle that gave the Union control of Missouri and northern Arkansas.[124]

The day before the battle, Colonel Vandever marched a detachment of General Curtis's army, including his Ninth Iowa Infantry, forty-one miles from Huntsville, Arkansas, to Sugar Creek, Arkansas, in sixteen hours with only two fifteen-minute stops.[125] It was a feat little seen since the days of Charlemagne. Both Vandever and Herron won distinction during the battle, for which the congressman-colonel would receive a generalship and Herron the Congressional Medal of Honor.

While Vandever and his regiment were marching from Fayetteville to Batesville, Arkansas, in April 1862, LeGrand Byington was in Washington,

D.C., meeting with Ohio congressman Vallandigham and other anti-Lincoln, antiwar Democrats who were strategizing his case, *Byington vs. Vandever*, that was coming up before the House Committee on Elections.[126]

On May 8, Representative George Browne of Rhode Island, a member of the Unionist Party, which wished to preserve the Union but did not align itself with Republicans or northern Democrats, brought to the floor of the House a recommended resolution from the Committee on Elections. It read, "Resolved, that William Vandever has not been entitled to a seat as a member of the House since he was mustered into the military service of the United States as colonel of the Ninth Iowa Volunteer Infantry, to wit: since the 24th day of September, A.D. 1861."[127] Nowhere in the resolution was LeGrand Byington or the contested election mentioned. Instead, the Committee on Elections preferred to focus on whether a member of Congress could simultaneously serve in the military or in any other government office.

Representative Elihu Washburne (R-IL) moved to postpone any discussion or vote on the resolution to December. Washburne pointed out that other House members who were serving in the military would be impacted by the resolution, including representatives from ten states—Illinois, Pennsylvania and New York, among others. Representative Henry Grider, a Unionist from Kentucky, agreed with postponement, believing the war would soon be over and "these gallant officers could then be here and be heard." The House of Representatives voted seventy-nine to forty-nine to postpone the matter until the third session began in December.[128]

Colonel Vandever was in the House that May and spoke in his defense, which was "very satisfactory," according to the *Washington National Republican*. Vandever had received a dispatch in Helena, Arkansas, from Washington that the resolution to remove him was coming to the floor of the House for debate.[129] While back in Congress, Vandever exercised the rights of a sitting member of Congress and recorded two votes, one on May 7 over a disputed election in Nebraska and the other on May 9 on HR374, which was related to providing freedom to those who were enslaved in U.S. territories.[130]

Colonel Vandever returned to Helena and spent the summer and fall on expedition in Arkansas with his regiment. On November 29, 1862, William Vandever was recognized for his bravery and leadership in the western theater of the war and promoted to brigadier general, U.S. Volunteers, and sent to command a brigade in the Army of the Tennessee.[131]

HOMETOWN POLITICS

In the summer of 1862, the editors of the *Dubuque Daily Herald* printed a letter from LeGrand Byington titled "The Congressman Colonel." In his letter, Byington accused Vandever of drawing $10,000 in pay as both a congressman and a colonel while neglecting his duty as a congressman, all in violation of article I of the Constitution.[132]

The *Dubuque Daily Herald* was managed by two seasoned Democratic newspaper editors who were active in local and state party politics. Dennis Mahony (pronounced ma-HAY-nee), the proprietor of the *Herald* since 1851, took on a new partner and coeditor in 1862.[133] Mahony's new coconspirator at the editorial desk was Stilson Hutchins, a Copperhead newspaperman who had most recently owned and published the *Iowa State Journal* in Des Moines. Hutchins removed to Dubuque from Des Moines to assist in publishing the *Dubuque Daily Herald*. In 1862, Hutchins purchased the *Herald* from Mahony and published it as the *Dubuque Democratic Herald* until 1865. Today, Stilson Hutchins is most noted for his relationship with Joseph Pulitzer and for founding the *Washington Post* in 1877.[134]

Mahony, Hutchins and the *Dubuque Daily Herald* acted as the primary organs for LeGrand Byington's efforts to flip the Republican congressional seat in Iowa. It was the *Herald* that first printed Byington's letters of accusation against Vandever. And in turn, Byington supported Dennis Mahony after his arrest by the Lincoln administration on August 14, 1862, and imprisonment in the Old Capital Prison in Washington, D.C., for discouraging military enlistments.[135] Mahony was never formally charged after his arrest, and with his writ of habeas corpus suspended by the Lincoln administration, he remained in federal prison through the election and until he swore allegiance to the Union in early November.

The arrest of Mahony by the Lincoln administration raised cries from Democrats across Iowa and the nation. Stilson Hutchins, who was active in his local Democratic Party, saw an opportunity to advance the cause he and Mahony had been fighting for and to ensure the spotlight remained on him and the newspaper he now had full editorial control over, the *Dubuque Daily Herald*.

Iowa was going through congressional redistricting in 1862 due to the 1860 census. The state was going from two to six congressional districts, and the city of Dubuque, represented by one of its own, William Vandever, was being assigned to a newly created Third District.[136] William Vandever decided not to run for reelection for the Second Congressional District of Iowa, nor did he decide to run for the newly created Third District to continue to represent his hometown of Dubuque. Vandever chose to stay in the military and serve out the remainder of his second term in Congress.

Stilson Hutchins, the chair of the Third District Democratic Convention of 1862, was able to get his business partner and political cohort nominated for the district's congressional seat in a split convention. Mahony beat his opponent fifty-two two-thirds votes to fifty-one one-third votes, with several Democratic newspapers in the district refusing to endorse the nomination while Mahony still sat in Old Capital Prison in Washington, D.C., awaiting charges of treason that would never come.[137]

The Iowa Republican Party nominated William Boyd Allison of Dubuque for the Third Congressional District, and replacing William Vandever in the Second District was Davenport Republican Hiram Price.[138] Not surprisingly, LeGrand Byington did not try for the nomination for the Second District seat held by Vandever. In paying his debt of gratitude, Byington agreed to stump the Third District on behalf of Mahony when Byington was not working on his plea before the Committee on Elections in the U.S. House of Representatives to unseat Vandever.[139]

On October 14, 1862, Dubuque Republican William Boyd Allison beat imprisoned Democratic newspaper editor Dennis Mahony in an election to become the first representative to serve in Iowa's newly formed Third Congressional District. Davenport's Hiram Price beat the Democratic newspaper editor of the *Muscatine Courier*, Edward H. Thayer, for the right to replace outgoing Second District congressman William Vandever upon the expiration of his term on March 3, 1863.[140]

The federal elections in the fall of 1862 did not trigger a withdrawal of the recommended resolution by the House Committee on Elections regarding *Byington v. Vandever*, which was still up for consideration in December. The discussion had larger implications than who succeeded Vandever in his congressional seat. It also had implications on other congressmen serving in the military, which, if they were also expelled, could see several Republican seats potentially turn Democratic. No less than nineteen congressmen, fifteen Republicans and four Democrats, from at least ten states, were serving in the military between 1861 and 1863 while holding on to their seats in Congress.[141]

A Question of Honor

For Vandever, the accusations of him receiving double pay had, in part, turned into a question of honor, and for that reason, Vandever found himself back in Washington, D.C., in early December. The Washington correspondent for the *Burlington Hawkeye* reported on December 13 that Vandever had arrived in Washington a few days prior and was certain to be unseated along with the other congressmen who were serving in the army.[142]

On December 11, Congressman Vandever again exercised his right as a sitting member of Congress and joined a majority of his fellow representatives in voting "yea" on a motion to shelve a proposed resolution declaring Lincoln's Emancipation Proclamation "an assumption of power dangerous to the rights of citizens and the perpetuity of freedom."[143] When Vandever learned the resolution to declare his seat vacated would not come up for debate and vote for another month, he returned to the war.

On January 20, 1863, the House of Representatives took up the case of William Vandever, "a representative holding a commission in the army and a seat in the House," according to Davenport, Iowa's *Daily Democrat and News*.[144] The case against Vandever started as an effort by LeGrand Byington to evict and replace Vandever in Iowa's Second District House seat. The case moved beyond Byington once the official October 1862 Iowa election occurred, and Hiram Price and William Boyd Allison were elected respectively to the Iowa Second and Third Congressional District seats for the Thirty-Eighth U.S. Congress. The case then became about all the then-current congressmen who were also serving in the army and whether they would all be forced to resign one of their offices of trust within the U.S. government or be expelled from Congress.

Bringing the question regarding the Vandever case to the floor, Chairman Henry Dawes (R-MA) from the Committee on Elections reiterated the recommended resolution on January 20. Mr. Dawes argued the question at hand came down to two factors. First, Vandever had drawn dual pay in his duties as a member of Congress and as an officer in the military. Second, the duties of a member of Congress and a military officer were so diverse that they could not be performed by the same person.[145]

Representative Washburne of Illinois once again moved to postpone the discussion of Vandever's removal, this time to February. Washburne noted that recently promoted Brigadier General Vandever had engaged in the assault and capture of Fort Hindman near Arkansas Post and could not be in Washington until February to address the charges of dual pay and dual service then at the forefront of his case. Washburne, a close friend of President Lincoln and General Grant, was undoubtedly in regular communication with his fellow Republican Vandever. Washburne, like Grant, was from Galena, Illinois, just fifteen miles from Vandever's home in Dubuque, Iowa. Both men knew many of the same businessmen and politicians from these two intertwined Mississippi River Valley lead mining towns.[146]

Washburne lost his bid to postpone the discussion, and the proposed resolution was adopted, declaring Vandever had not been entitled to his seat in the House since the time he was mustered into military service in September 1861. Representative Horace Maynard, a border state Unionist from Tennessee, asked whether the resolution amounted to expulsion, which constitutionally requires a two-thirds vote by the House. Speaker Colfax overruled debate of the question, concluding it did not amount to expulsion. Mr. Maynard appealed the decision by the speaker, and the adopted resolution was deferred pending the appeal.[147] Vandever's case was not dead, and Congressman Vandever still had full privileges as a member of the U.S. House of Representatives.

The *Lancaster Examiner* reported on the follow-up debate in the House on January 21 over Mr. Maynard's appeal of the speaker's decision. During the appeal discussion, the vote by the Committee on Elections that initially passed the resolution onto the full House was called into question, and the whole question of the resolution was opened back up to debate. It was ultimately agreed to by the House to postpone any final vote on the committee resolution or the appeal until March 3.[148] Vandever's trusted associates, Representative Elihu Washburne (R-IL) and fellow Iowa representative James F. Wilson (R-IA), offered a number of motions that ultimately led to the resolution being postponed to March 3, the last day of Vandever's second term in Congress.[149] This effectually killed the Committee on Elections' resolution that declared Vandever ineligible for his congressional seat beginning from the date of his mustering into military service on September 24, 1861, thus allowing Congressman Vandever to server out his second term.[150]

General Vandever was not present to defend himself during the January 20–21, 1863 House debates over *Byington v. Vandever*. Vandever's fellow Iowan representative James Wilson spoke on behalf of his colleague and pointed out that Vandever had returned his military pay. It was also noted that section 6 of the 1856 Act to Regulate the Compensation of Members of Congress stipulated that congressmen only get paid for the days in each session they attend. The act requires the House sergeant in arms to deduct from each

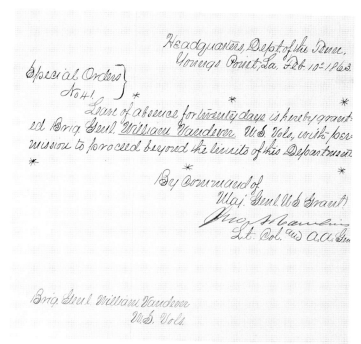

Special Order No. 41, granting General Vandever twenty days to travel to Washington, D.C., to complete his term in Congress, February 10, 1863. *Author's collection.*

congressman's salary the pay for each day they are reported absent during a session.[151]

Congressman Vandever had one last opportunity to address the accusations of accepting dual pay during the scheduled debate on March 3. On February 10, Special Order No. 41 was issued, giving General Vandever a twenty-day furlough to leave the military district of the Army of the Tennessee to travel to Washington, D.C., to join the Thirty-Seventh Congress one last time.[152]

On February 14, the House was once again obliged to debate *Byington v. Vandever* based on a last-minute effort by Representative Samuel Cox of Ohio and the Copperhead Democrats to get one of their own into Vandever's seat. Representative Cox proposed a new resolution regarding Vandever to the Committee on Elections' chairman Dawes, who brought the proposed resolution to the floor of the House. Mr. Cox's new resolution stated that LeGrand Byington was duly elected and outright won the seat vacated by Vandever when he joined the military. The House voted down the new Cox resolution and discharged the Committee on Elections from any further consideration in the matter of *Byington v. Vandever.*[153]

General Vandever was in Washington, D.C., to close out his term in the Thirty-Seventh U.S. Congress. His last vote as an Iowa congressman was recorded on February 25, 1863, on a bill to enroll the national forces. Vandever's last vote was in support of the war effort and gave President Lincoln the power to draft "all able-bodied White male citizens of the United States between the ages of twenty and forty-five years, except as hereinafter excepted, and are hereby declared to constitute the militia of the United States, and shall be liable to perform military duty in the service of the United States when called out by the president for that purpose in the manner authorized by law."[154]

On March 3, 1863, the final gavel fell, closing out the Thirty-Seventh Session of the United States Congress with William Vandever still listed as the sitting member from Iowa's Second Congressional District. Congressman Vandever had served out his second term in its entirety, despite efforts by LeGrand Byington, Representative Samuel Cox and others.[155]

LATER LIFE

Vandever would go on to serve as brigadier general until the end of the Civil War, marching with General Sherman through Georgia and the Carolinas. General Vandever was with General Sherman when Confederate general Joe Johnston surrendered his army near Bentonville, North Carolina, at the end of the war. After the war, Vandever returned to Dubuque, where he once again practiced law until 1875, when he entered service as inspector of U.S. Indian Agents under his former commander and then president, U.S. Grant. Inspector Vandever would fail in his valiant efforts to prevent the approaching war on the Sioux in 1875 and 1876.

In 1884, Vandever moved from Dubuque to California and was once again elected to the U.S. House of Representatives for the Fiftieth and Fifty-First U.S. Congresses from the state of California. The venerable "congressman-colonel" William Vandever died at his home in Ventura, California, on July 23, 1893, at the age of seventy-six.[156]

SANCTIONED SIMULTANEOUS SERVICE

It is yet to be discovered why President Lincoln, Secretary of War Stanton, Speaker of the House Colfax and General Grant continued to allow Colonel and later General Vandever to leave his military post in the western theater to travel to Washington, D.C., for the second and third sessions of the Thirty-Seventh U.S. Congress. Surely, they knew article I of the U.S. Constitution prohibited individuals from simultaneously holding two positions within the U.S. government. Perhaps Lincoln felt a congressman who was also serving in the army was no different than him—serving as the elected president as well as the commander-in-chief of the military—and did not feel it applied in this situation at this time. Perhaps Lincoln did not consider a military commission as holding a government office.

Speaker Colfax had to have been aware of the debate within his house of Congress regarding the conflict in Vandever's service and the service of over a dozen other members and their importance to the nation in its hour of need as both congressmen and military officers. Although Colfax did seemingly agree with the original resolution to, in essence, remove Vandever from the seat he continued to occupy, was that done based on principal or House procedure?

President Lincoln and Secretary Stanton, along with General Grant, approved of General Vandever's several trips from the western front during the Civil War to Washington, D.C., to participate in House proceedings as an elected official. On February 23, 1863, Vandever specifically requested a twenty-day extension from the secretary of war and wrote on his military leave document, "I find it important to remain…in this city as my official term as member of the House is about to expire." Secretary Stanton, recognizing that Vandever's request was as much a political request as it was a military request, did not approve, deny or write a response on the document that started out as military Special Order No. 41. Instead, Stanton passed the request on to the president, who wrote on the document on February 24, "Let the leave of absence be extended twenty additional days. A. Lincoln."[157]

It is clear William Vandever did not resign his seat in Congress when he entered military service as the colonel of the Ninth Iowa Infantry on September 24, 1861. And the congressional record is clear that the resolution from the House Committee on Elections to remove Vandever from his seat on constitutional grounds never came to a final vote, as it expired on March 3, 1863.

The most logical reason President Lincoln supported Vandever's simultaneous service and the simultaneous service of other U.S. congressmen who were also acting as military officers in the war, like Senator and Brigadier General James H. Lane of Kansas, was the precarious balance of power in both houses of the U.S. Congress at the time and the sentiment and southern

V. 135. C.B. '63

File with V. 90. C.B. '66
House of Reps.
Febry. 23? 1863
Hon. J. W. Stanton.
Secy of War.
I respectfully ask
an extension of the within
leave for twenty days—I find
it important to remain about
time in this city—as my offi-
cial term as a member of the
House is about to expire
Very Respty
Wm Vandever

Let this leave of ab-
sence be extended twenty
additional days.
A. Lincoln
February 24. 1863.
S.O.95. Par 6.

Reverse, Special-Order No.
41, granting General Vandever
twenty additional days leave by
President Lincoln to finish his
term in Congress, February 24,
1864. *Author's collection.*

sympathies that existed at the same time in states like Iowa and Kansas.[158] Had Vandever been removed or resigned in 1861, there was a chance that a Copperhead Democrat like LeGrand Byington or newspaper editor Dennis Mahony would have taken his place in Congress, making it that much more difficult for Lincoln to execute a war that was just getting underway and that many Americans wished to avoid at all costs.

Lincoln was not going to take a chance on losing Republican-held seats in either house of Congress, upsetting an already delicate balance of power. Lincoln and men like Vandever were willing to do whatever it took to preserve the Union. A constitutional duty going back to the Articles of Confederation and Perpetual Union and something that Lincoln believed was a higher duty than enforcing section 6 of article I concerning holding multiple federal offices or enforcing the writ of habeas corpus or other infringements on liberty he felt necessary in the nation's hour of need to execute the war toward his highest constitutional duty: the preservation of the Union.

That is why President Lincoln and members of the Senate and House of Representatives permitted men like William Vandever and the other eighteen-plus congressmen to simultaneously serve in Congress and in the military during the uncertainty of the early years of the nation's darkest hours.

4

FREDERICK DOUGLASS

Portrait by Samuel Root

*I*mmediately after the end of the American Civil War, in 1865, U.S. president Andrew Johnson and the Republican-controlled U.S. Congress turned their attention to implementing the late President Abraham Lincoln's southern Reconstruction policies. President Johnson, along with the Democrats and conservative Republicans in Congress, wanted a quick path to Reconstruction through pardons and the absolution of the southern states. At the same time, the "Radical Republicans" in the United States, including Dubuque's own U.S. representative William Boyd Allison, were pushing for harsher terms for southern states and those who participated in the Confederacy during the recent Civil War.[159]

As American cities in both the North and South began to settle back into life without war, the Young Men's Literary Association of Dubuque, Iowa, sponsored the city's Winter Course of Lectures program.[160]

As the midwestern and western United States were being settled throughout the nineteenth century, one of the first forms of community entertainment that also provided a platform for community discussion of important topics of the day, as well as for speeches of an intellectual nature, was the local theater and lyceum, or lecture hall.

Dubuque's Young Men's Literary Association sponsored such speakers as German revolutionary and Union general Carl Schurz, who was an eastern newspaper editor at the time of his visit; New England abolitionist attorney Wendell Phillips; and "Old Man Eloquent," Frederick Douglass, the Black abolitionist and suffragist.[161]

Frederick Douglass, Dubuque,
April 19, 20 or 21, 1866.
*Photographer, Samuel Root; Gilder
Lehrman Institute.*

Frederick Douglass, a celebrated orator, author and formerly enslaved person who "stole himself" from bondage, appeared in Dubuque no less than three times between 1865 and 1870 as he traveled the national lecture circuit. Douglass first spoke in Dubuque on April 20, 1866.[162] At the time, he was lecturing on the need for a favorable Reconstruction and Black suffrage. President Johnson had vetoed the Freedmen's Bureau Bill on February 18, 1866, just two months earlier. The nation began speaking about the impeachment of a president. And Frederick Douglass, the "great agitator," a label he believed to be a call of duty, had a few thoughts on these matters that he wished to share with anyone who would listen. And they did listen.

Many progressive citizens of Dubuque, including Austin Adams, a founding member of Dubuque's Young Men's Literary Association, and his wife, Mrs. Mary Newbury Adams, were surely delighted to hear that Douglass was coming to Dubuque.[163] Others in the city were not as excited. The *Dubuque Daily Herald*, a local Democratic paper that was anti-Lincoln during the war and anti-Reconstruction after the war, was sarcastic in its judgment of Douglass's visit on the front page of its April 21, 1866 edition. The paper's sharp jabs were targeted at the local White progressive citizens as much as it was the "Negro" Douglass.

> *In Dubuque, Fred, who is not such a bad fellow, and a heap better than most of those who, claiming to be white, now mourn that they were not black men not taken to the bosom of a radical family. The speculative gentlemen who exhibited him last evening at Julien Hall, considerately provided for him at the public hotel, making a special contract for so many rations and such an amount of lodging. Everybody stops at hotels, and why should not Fred Douglass, but then you will say the African man and brother should receive especial care having been rendered so helpless by emancipation.*[164]

The *Herald* knew Douglass was a paid orator sponsored by local "speculative gentlemen," event sponsors or literary associations—whatever the case may be—and as such would have his full expenses paid, including meals and lodging. This was not uncommon. Douglass was paid one hundred dollars by the event's sponsors, George D. Wood and his brother-in-law Hosea B. Baker.[165] Wood was the second vice-president of the Young Men's Literary Association in 1866.[166] Both men were active members of the First Congregational Church of Dubuque—an active supporter of Dubuque's Colored Christian Association in the 1860s—and would often help support worthy community projects and programs.[167]

The city of Dubuque, like most established, growing and politically active cities in America, had a Democratic- and a Republican-leaning newspaper that often told quite different sides of a story. In Dubuque, the *Dubuque Daily Herald* was the Democratic newspaper, and the *Dubuque Daily Times* was the Republican newspaper.[168] The *Dubuque Daily Herald*, a racist newspaper by twenty-first-century standards, held views more in line with southern Democrat newspapers of the time.

The *Daily Herald*, like most American newspapers at that time, would refer to Black Americans, including Douglass, as a "Negro," "colored" or, sometimes, "black" throughout its pages, using general terms of the day. When the *Daily Herald* wished to stick Douglass or other Black Americans with a verbal dagger, however, it would maliciously refer to him as a "darkey" or "nigger" in its pages, as it did after Douglass spoke in Manchester, Iowa, in 1867. These hateful words were used throughout the *Daily Herald*'s pages before, during and long after the Civil War.[169]

So, it probably came as a surprise to many of the *Daily Herald*'s readers when its article on Douglass's first visit almost sounded sincere, even if fleeting, when it said Douglass was "not such a bad fellow." That was the desired effect the *Dubuque Daily Times* hoped Douglass would have on many of the readers of the *Daily Herald* who might come hear him speak, doing away with many of the misconceptions about Black men and their abilities compared to those of their White counterparts by seeing Douglass's humanity in the flesh. In a brief article in its April 15 edition, the *Daily Times* proclaimed, "Fred. Douglass is to lecture in Dubuque on Friday evening next, April 20th. This will be a welcome announcement to many of our readers. His presence will do away with many prejudices that have been sincerely held against him and his race."[170] Indeed, this was the effect Douglass desired as well.

In the *Daily Herald*'s main article following the Douglass lecture, it opened with a sarcastic comparison of the Douglass lecture to a "side show" of the play *Uncle Tom's Cabin*, which was being performed the same night as Douglass's lecture at Dubuque's premier theater and lecture hall, the Athenaeum, at the corner of Fourth and Main Streets. Because the Athenaeum was already committed, Douglass spoke that night at Julien Hall, the same building where the Young Men's Literary Association was located, at Fifth and Locust Streets. Dubuque's own William Vandever, a former U.S. congressman turned Union general in the late war, introduced Douglass.[171]

The *Daily Herald* did not agree with Douglass's premise that the country was in another crisis due to President Johnson "and that the strength of the country was again being put forth," an assertion the *Herald* called a farce. After mocking Douglass's belief that enfranchising Black Americans was a key to a successful Reconstruction, the *Dubuque Daily Herald* did fulfill a very small portion of the *Daily Times*'s fervent wish that Douglass's "presence will do away with many prejudices that have been sincerely held against him and his race" with the remaining portion of its article.[172]

The *Herald* article goes on to cautiously praise Douglass, the man, while, at the same time, it continues to point out its belief that he is incorrect in his position. "Without doubt, Mr. Douglass is the ablest champion of the colored race in this or any country. He is an earnest speaker and as such necessarily eloquent, not always candid but as he speaks in his own interest, much of his lack in this respect may readily be pardoned." The article goes on to conclude:

We commend his lecture as being nearer a logical and consistent argument than any politician pretending philanthropy can offer. Fred Douglass, with enough of the Negro blood in his veins to identify him with the black race, and the talent and honesty to make him a peer among men, is the most powerful champion of Negro suffrage in the nation, and the American people may without difficulty be induced to grant to him what they would unhesitatingly refuse to any other standing in his stead.[173]

In 1868, the self-made Douglass once again graced the lecture halls of Dubuque to give his by-then-famous speech on what it takes to be a "Self-Made Man." On March 3, 1868, Douglass performed his oration at the Athenaeum at Fourth and Main Streets.[174] Douglass had first given this well-received speech in 1859 and had performed it periodically since.[175]

Tickets for the program were sold at local bookstores for fifty and seventy-five cents each. The box office profits from the event went to Dubuque's Colored Christian Association, a local African Methodist

Episcopal organization with thirty-nine members in 1864. The Colored Christian Association was affiliated with the Young Men's Christian Association of Dubuque and supported by different congregations of faith around the city. According to the *Daily Herald*, the speech was well attended and well received.[176]

The third and last time Frederick Douglass was known to have lectured in Dubuque occurred on March 1, 1869, at the Athenaeum. His lecture was on "William the Silent." The *Dubuque Daily Times*'s review of the lecture was not pleasing. "The lecture was a long, prosey [*sic*], disconnected harangue about the 80-year religious war in the Netherlands, with a meagre reference to William of Orange!" Calling the speech "a bore," the *Times* declared, "Mr. Douglass may lecture well of those things that touches him and nearly, but as a historical lecturer, he is not a success."[177] Douglass clearly failed in his attempt to parallel the Dutch struggle for religious liberty to the then-recent American struggles over emancipation.[178]

Not much else is known about Frederick Douglass's visits to Dubuque, what he said in any of his lectures or his interactions with Dubuque citizens, apart from those he had with Samuel Root, a nationally known portrait and landscape photographer living in Dubuque, Iowa, since 1857.[179]

Frederick Douglass sought out photographers wherever and whenever he could, making him the most photographed person of the nineteenth century. Douglass knew that if more White Americans could hear and see a real Black man, not just a caricature in a story or an engraving in the newspaper, it would help them understand and acknowledge the humanity of his race. By going to local photographers, especially well-known photographers, Douglass knew his image would be sold as a curiosity and would be seen far and wide. He had hoped it might engage people in discussions on race, enfranchisement and racial equality for Black Americans.[180]

Samuel Root was the kind of photographer a person like Douglass would have sought out upon reaching a bustling city in the northwest like Dubuque. Samuel Root and his older brother Marcus Aurelius were well-known Daguerreian photographers who made names for themselves in Philadelphia and New York City between 1846 and 1857. Samuel Root had taken well-known daguerreotypes of numerous famous people in Philadelphia and New York, including Vice President George Dallas, writer George W. Curtis, theologian Albert Barnes, the singer "Swedish Nightingale" Jenny Lind, poet Bayard Taylor, statesman Henry Clay,

Above, left: Henry Clay, senator of Kentucky. Clay said this image was "decidedly the best… likeness I have ever had taken." *Photographers, M.A.&S. Root, 1848; Hindman Auctions.*

Above, right: Franklin Pierce; this image was used in Pierce's presidential campaign, 1852. *Photographer, Samuel Root; Hindman Auctions.*

Opposite: Showman P.T. Barnum with his newly discovered star Charles Stratton, also known as General Tom Thumb, circa 1850. *Photographer, Samuel Root; National Portrait Gallery.*

presidential candidate Franklin Pierce, artist Rembrandt Peale and General Tom Thumb while he was standing on a table leaning on the shoulder of circus showman extraordinaire P.T. Barnum.[181]

There is a good chance the Root brothers worked together when composing the image of Henry Clay, as it is often attributed to both men. Samuel Root had one of the seven "Root" daguerreotypes taken of Clay in his possession upon his death. The original daguerreotype of Franklin Pierce, often attributed to M.A. Root, was recently sold at auction. The piece was discovered to contain a matte stamped "S. Root, 563 Broadway, N.Y." The image of P.T. Barnum and Tom Thumb is most likely from Samuel Root, too. Root's gallery in New York was close to Barnum's American Museum. Barnum was responsible for bringing Jenny Lind to America and Bayard Taylor, who authored a poem about Lind for a Barnum competition; both were photographed by Samuel Root.

Root took photographs in Dubuque of Methodist bishop Matthew Simpson, President Lincoln's spiritual advisor; Civil War general Francis Herron; and suffragist-orator Frederick Douglass.[182]

A carte-de-visite of the image Root produced of Douglass is kept in the Gilder Lehrman Institute of American History in New York City, and it includes the artist's stamp on the back, which states, "S. Root, *Photographer* 166 Main Street, Dubuque, Iowa."[183] It has been written that the carte-de-visite photograph of Frederick Douglass was taken by Samuel Root at his studio in Dubuque sometime between 1865 and 1880.[184]

Root moved his studio and his home from 166 Main Street in late 1867.[185] Given the facts that Douglass spoke in Dubuque in 1866, 1868 and 1869 and that Root moved his studio from 166 Main Street in late 1867, it reasons that Root took the carte-de-visite portrait of Douglass in Dubuque during

THE DAGUERREOTYPIST.

Left: *The Daguerreotypist*, featuring brothers Marcus and Samuel Root, famous early American photographers, 1849. *Author's collection.*

Below: Methodist bishop Matthew Simpson, the namesake of Simpson College in Iowa. *Photographer, Samuel Root, Dubuque, September 16, 1868; author's collection.*

Root & Cutter's, northeast corner of Eighth and Main Streets, Dubuque. Root moved here from the southeast corner of Eighth and Main Streets in late 1867. *Author's collection.*

his 1866 speech on Reconstruction. It is likely Douglass had the picture taken on April 19, 20 or 21, 1866.

It is known with certainty from the local newspapers that Douglass was in Dubuque on the day he gave his speech, April 20. It is also known from the newspapers that Douglass departed Dubuque on the 10:00 a.m. train the following day, April 21, as he headed to Anamosa, Iowa, for another lecture that evening.[186] It is unclear whether Douglass arrived in Dubuque on April 19, the day before the scheduled Dubuque lecture, or on the twentieth, the day of his lecture. The most likely scenario is that Douglass arrived in Dubuque on one of the morning trains on April 20. After finding his hotel and the lecture hall, Douglass probably walked the three blocks or so to Eighth and Main Streets to sit for his portrait with Samuel Root, who was assuredly happy to oblige. It is unknown whether Douglass sought out Root or Root sought out Douglass to sit for the "picture-making," as Douglass was fond of calling it.[187] Nor is it known if Douglass and Root knew each other prior to their meeting in Dubuque in 1866.

The image taken of Douglass by Samuel Root that day shows a man who is impeccably dressed with a serious, stern look on his brow and a light, relaxed grip on his gold-handled walking stick, suggesting to the viewer this is a proud, confident man who is sure of himself and his cause. He is man who knows his every move is watched and scrutinized, as others look for faults they can ascribe to his entire race. He is man who sits with the pressures of a righteous might he knows is guided by a higher and larger hand than his own. Root's image of Douglass is one of the finer remaining images of Douglass. It is a well-exposed image with a clarity and crispness that brings depth to Douglass, the man, and this could only have been achieved by an expert photographer like Samuel Root.

In 1895, Frederick Douglass met up with Samuel Root one last time when he was laid to rest in Mount Hope Cemetery in his former adoptive hometown of Rochester, New York. Samuel Root was laid to rest next to his wife in her family's plot in Mount Hope Cemetery six years earlier.[188]

5

THE NATIONAL MILITARY ENCAMPMENT OF 1884

In the spring of 1884, Dubuque, Iowa, was alive with military splendor as it played host to the largest military encampment in the United States since the end of the Civil War. Dubuque, a city of 22,254 inhabitants in 1880, prepared for 20,000 to 30,000 visitors who were expected to descend on the Mississippi River town to watch the events of the encampment that were being held at the fairgrounds, north of the city.[189]

For the first time, military units from the federal army and from the state's national guard rendezvoused in Dubuque from June 16 to 21, 1884, to participate in joint military drilling, drill competitions and a large "sham" battle at the close of the encampment.

Parades were held throughout the week, with the main procession of soldiers in the grand parade on Tuesday, June 17, stretching down Main Street from First Street all the way to Seventeenth Street. Music filled the air throughout the week from military bands parading about town. Flags and red-white-and-blue bunting decorated city hall and several city firehouses. The office of Henderson, Hurd and Daniels at 608 Main Street displayed an old Civil War battle flag that was provided by Colonel David B. Henderson, who was a nationally known Civil War veteran in his second year as a U.S. congressman from Iowa.[190]

Cavalry members from Milwaukee and St. Louis rode their fine steeds in the grand parade. Eleven different artillery units from as far away as New Orleans joined the encampment, with thirty cannon and artillery pieces present for the sham battle. The Fourth and Fifth U.S. Artillery were both on hand with heavy cannon. The Clinton (Iowa) Gun Squad brought a cannon that was captured from Confederate forces at Vicksburg during the late Civil War, and it was used during the sham battle.[191]

Twelve different infantry units from around the country made up the bulk of the men encamped at the fairgrounds in makeshift regimental barracks and tent campsites. The Fourth U.S. Infantry was the lead federal infantry unit that was encamped. The present militia and infantry units from different states' national guards included the Mobile Rifles from Alabama; the Tredway Rifles of the Third Missouri Infantry; the National Rifles from Washington, D.C.; and the Busch Zouaves from St. Louis, Missouri. Seven military bands and four drum corps, including a Dubuque drum corps, provided music for drilling, marching, parades, concerts, dancing and the sham battle, and they could be heard all around town.[192]

The Third Missouri Infantry had history with the city of Dubuque dating to the start of the Civil War. The Third Missouri, Company I, was composed of Iowa soldiers who were originally recruited into service in Dubuque in 1861 for the Lyon Regiment, Nineteenth Missouri Infantry. The Nineteenth Missouri merged with the Third Missouri Infantry shortly after it was mustered into service. All the Dubuque, Waverly, Dyersville and eastern Iowa boys who came from the Nineteenth Missouri were assigned to Company I.[193] A notable member of the Tredway Rifles at the Dubuque encampment was the nineteen-year-old son of General William Tecumseh Sherman, Philemon Tecumseh Sherman.[194]

Joint encampments of states' national guard units were not uncommon in 1884, and a large national encampment of national guardsmen from multiple states was held in 1883 in Nashville, Tennessee. The Nashville encampment was led by Brigadier General C.S. Bentley of the Iowa National Guard. In 1884, military drilling and instruction did not follow a consistent nationwide standard. Encampments were a way to bring different units from around a state or region together to share ideas and techniques and to become more cohesive in the event that they be called together in service of a larger cause. Some state guard units drilled using outdated techniques from the Civil War. Some units were made up of members of German descent and used Prussian drill techniques. Other units used modern techniques and tactics. Over time, federal and national guard officers saw the need for greater cooperation and believed joint encampments were a way to start standardizing drill techniques, share information and build a working relationship between the federal army and the collective states' national guards.

A big proponent of a joint federal-state encampment was Dubuque resident, Civil War veteran and commander of the "Northwest Brigade" of the Iowa National Guard, Brigadier General C.S. Bentley. General Bentley was elected chairman of the Dubuque encampment's Committee of Arrangements and worked long and hard to organize every aspect of the national gathering.[195] General Bentley was already nationally known for organizing successful national guard encampments, including the prior year's interstate encampment in Nashville, Tennessee.

Assisting Brigadier General Bentley with the Dubuque encampment by order of Secretary of War Robert Todd Lincoln was Captain William H. Powell of the Fourth U.S. Infantry out of Fort Omaha, Nebraska.[196] Captain Powell was a career military man going back to the start of the Civil War, where he saw action in the eastern theater at the Second Battle of Bull Run and the Battles of Antietam, Fredericksburg and Gettysburg. Upon Powell's arrival in Dubuque, he immediately took over preparations for the camp at the fairgrounds and started to plan for the sham battle that was scheduled to take place at the end of the encampment.

Military observers and other honored guests were among the thousands of spectators who came to Dubuque to see the great military gathering. Retired career military officer and Confederate general E. Kirby Smith was on hand as a guest of Dubuque resident William Andrew. General Winfield Scott Hancock, who gained national fame at the Battle of Gettysburg and as the Democratic Party's 1880 nominee for president of the United States, was invited but had to regrettably turn down the invitation due to a prior engagement.[197] Governor Rusk of Wisconsin and Governor Sherman of Iowa both made appearances at the encampment. *Harper's Weekly*, a nationally distributed journal of the time, asked General Bentley to hire a local artisan photographer to capture images of the encampment for the magazine. Bentley turned to local Dubuque war artist Alexander Simplot. Simplot gained a national reputation during the first half of the Civil War with his sketches from Grant's army in the western theater, including the first published pictures related to the Civil War, which appeared in the May 25, 1861 edition of *Harper's Weekly*. Other photographers from around the Midwest attended the encampment, including Dubuque photographer Samuel Root and St. Louis photographer John A. Hazenstab.[198]

Additional military observers who were on hand for the national encampment included General John Gibbon of the Seventh U.S. Infantry, the acting commander of the Department of the Platte; Colonel William P. Carlin of the Fourth U.S. Infantry from Fort Omaha; Colonel John E. Smith

Images of the National Encampment, *Harper's Weekly*, July 1884, based on sketches by Dubuque's famed Civil War artist Alexander Simplot. *Author's collection.*

of the Fourth U.S. Infantry (retired); Colonel E.C. Mason of the Fourth U.S. Infantry and inspector general of the Department of the Platte; Lieutenant Colonel D.W. Flagler, the commander of Rock Island Arsenal; and the adjutant generals of Iowa, Missouri and Minnesota. Also in attendance was Major George Clitherall of the Alabama National Guard (retired), a founding member of the Mobile Rifles in 1836.[199]

General Gibbon's attendance offered him the opportunity for a reunion of sorts in Dubuque with an old Civil War brigade he used to command, the Black Hat Brigade, which was made up of regiments from Wisconsin, Michigan and Indiana. The Black Hat Brigade included five companies of men from across the Mississippi River from Dubuque in Grant County, Wisconsin. Companies C and I of the Second Wisconsin Infantry and Companies C, F and H of the Seventh Wisconsin Infantry were Grant County boys who were part of Gibbon's brigade that would go on to be immortalized as the Iron Brigade.[200]

General Gibbon saw action with the Iron Brigade up to and including the Battle of Antietam before being promoted. Gibbon participated in the

Battles of Fredericksburg, Chancellorsville and Gettysburg, among others. In November 1863, Gibbon attended the dedication of the Gettysburg National Cemetery, where he heard President Lincoln deliver his celebrated address. Gibbon would finish out the Civil War in the front parlor of Wilmer McLean at Appomattox Courthouse in Virginia. There, Confederate general Robert E. Lee surrendered to Union general Ulysses S. Grant. Gibbon would go on to participate in the Indian Wars of the 1860s and 1870s and was in command of the Seventh U.S. Infantry when it arrived just in time to bury the dead the day after Lieutenant Colonel George Armstrong Custer lost his battle in the Big Horn Valley in Montana, just eight years prior to the encampment.[201] With the possible exception of E. Kirby Smith, Gibbon was the most notable military observer at the Dubuque encampment.

The Dubuque Driving Park and Fairgrounds, north of the city heading out Couler Avenue (present-day Central Avenue), was selected by the encampment's Committee of Arrangements as the location in which to house the soldiers, hold the military drilling and conduct the sham battle. On the first day of the encampment, General Order No. 1 from General Bentley proclaimed, "The national encampment at Dubuque will be known as Camp Henderson" in honor of Dubuque's Colonel David B. Henderson.[202] Henderson, as a member of the U.S. House of Representatives, along with fellow Dubuque citizen U.S. senator William B. Allison, aided in the efforts to make the joint federal-state encampment in Dubuque a reality.[203] They left it up to fellow Dubuquer General Bentley to make the encampment a success.

Camp Henderson, Dubuque Driving Park and Fairgrounds, 1884. *Photographer, Samuel Root; author's collection.*

The scheduled program for the encampment consisted of daily guard mounting and dress parades accompanied by military bands performing for the crowds. The events of Tuesday, June 17, would consist of a grand citywide military parade followed by various company drilling exercises. The events of Wednesday, June 18, would have consisted of competitive drilling of the various infantry, had the day not been rained out. The events of Thursday, June 19, consisted of flying artillery drills and Gatling gun practice and ended with cavalry drills and a band concert. On Friday, June 20, the sham battle and assault on Fort Dubuque would occur, bringing the National Military Encampment to a near close.[204]

During the week, the drilling competitions resulted in Company F of the First Alabama Infantry, better known as the Mobile Rifles, winning first prize for the infantry competitive drills. The prize consisted of a gold-enameled badge for each member of the winning company.[205] The Busch Zouaves of Saint Louis, Missouri, won the Zouave competitive drill. The prize was a "unique ice-water set" of silver. Inscribed on it was "First Premium won by the Busch Zouaves, Dubuque, Iowa, June 16th, 1884."[206] The Milwaukee Light-Horse Squadron won the prize for the cavalry competitive drill. The prize consisted of a trophy that was eighteen inches in diameter and made of silver, bronze and other metals. Inscribed was "To the best-drilled cavalry company; Dubuque, June 1884."[207]

The Gatling gun demonstration by Skipwith's Battery from St. Louis consisted of 4,800 rounds being fired in one minute from four different guns to the delight of all who saw or heard. The drills and demonstrations were brought to a thunderous close with rapid maneuvers performed by Light Battery D of the Fifth U.S. Artillery and Light Battery F of the Fourth U.S. Artillery. The Washington Artillery from New Orleans, Louisiana, included in its ranks Dudley Selph, who was widely considered the best long-distance shot in North America and Europe.[208] The company won the artillery competitive drill, and its prize was a silver ice-water set.[209]

With the demonstration and competitive drilling complete, Friday, June 20, brought the highlight of the week—the sham battle. The object of the sham battle was to either assault or defend Fort Dubuque, depending on whose command you were assigned to. Fort Dubuque was a makeshift triangular fort with each side measuring one hundred feet in length and four feet in height. The fort was located at the crest of a prominent hill to the north of Camp Henderson at the intersection of two valleys. The fort was guarded by two three-inch guns and two twelve-pound howitzers.[210]

Captain Powell of the Fourth U.S. Infantry commanded the defensive forces of Fort Dubuque during the battle, and Lieutenant Colonel Mason,

ILLUST'D SWEET CAPORAL
PRIVATE; BUSCH ZOUAVES, ST. LOUIS, MO. MILITIA.

ILLUST'D SWEET CAPORAL
OFFICER, BUSCH ZOUAVES, ST. LOUIS, MO. MILITIA

Illustrated Sweet Caporal cigarette trading cards with a private and an officer of the St. Louis Busch Zouaves, circa 1887. *Author's collection.*

also of the Fourth U.S. Infantry, commanded the attacking forces. During the battle, the defenses put up a good fight, but eventually, Fort Dubuque inevitably fell, leaving Captain Powell no other choice but to blow up Fort Dubuque with fifty pounds of gun powder placed in a shaft in the ground located within the fort. Shortly after the grand explosion and the capture of the fort's flag, the Civil War regimental flag of the Ninth Iowa Infantry, the bloodless battle came to an end—and so did the day's festivities.[211]

The estimated twenty-thousand-plus spectators who came to Dubuque by train, boat, horse and on foot had experienced an action-packed week unlike anything Dubuque, or any midwestern city, had seen before.[212] The military encampment during peace time presented a carnival-like atmosphere for both soldier and spectator alike.

The daily events at Camp Henderson were not the only entertainment taking place on the fairgrounds. Set up at the north end of the grounds was a circus. Temporary gambling licenses were issued to numerous vendors. Some set up games of chance at the fairgrounds. Other local Dubuque establishments—namely, saloons—applied for gambling licenses and offered games of chance for the duration of the encampment. The local temperance movement, which believed vices like gambling and drink fed off one another, was not pleased. "The number of gambling licenses issued this present week is a matter of grave offense to a large majority," read the *Dubuque Daily Times*. Of greatest shame was "one of these gaming institutions" on Main Street between Sixth and Seventh Streets, which was "kept open day and night."[213] Captain Powell would later remark about the soldiers' conduct in Dubuque, "Although the camp was surrounded by saloons and drinking places of all kinds, I did not see a single soldier drunk or hear of a disorderly proceeding. To the presences and example of the regulars in this respect, I attribute much."[214]

For those who were less inclined towards vice, a gathering at a local private residence may have been more to their liking, or they may have taken in one of the many events that were happening in the evenings at the local roller-skating rinks or at the opera house. Clark's Rink on Main Street between Ninth & Tenth Streets held "war concerts" several nights in a row, with 150 "trained voices" singing patriotic songs. The performance included a "Negro quartette" that was "loudly encored time and again."[215] The Couler Avenue Rink on Couler Avenue (now Central Avenue), just north of Sanford Street, promoted the Jones sisters and their skate dancing. Their "grand march of the broom brigade" left the audiences rolling in laughter. On Thursday night, the Couler Avenue Rink held a large military ball. Both roller rinks had open skating for the public during the day and some evenings throughout the encampment.[216]

With so many visitors to the city and given the carnival-like atmosphere with open gambling all around, it is no surprise that the daily newspapers included individual stories of pickpockets and robberies. The June 22 edition of the *Dubuque Daily Times* listed the names and stories behind eleven different pickpockets nabbed in the act. Matthew Kirwin and John McLain were arrested for stealing a pocketbook from an attentive auditory. They were arrested by a soldier, Richard Robinson, of the Fourth U.S. Infantry and held until local police could take them. The Burke Light Guards also escorted two pickpockets to the "calaboose." Albert Carr observed a thief steeling a lady's gold watch and nabbed him by the neck in the amphitheater stands. The

The amphitheater at the Dubuque Driving Park and Fairgrounds, circa 1884. *Photographer, Samuel Root; Dubuque County Historical Society.*

thief struggled, and a fight ensued, involving the crowd. According to the *Dubuque Daily Times,* "A rope was produced, and the fellow would have been hung [*sic*] had not officers appeared."[217]

Aside from a few bad apples, the National Military Encampment at Dubuque was a success on all accounts. Many sang the praises of North and South working together in military harmony, pointing to the fact a former Confederate unit, the Washington Artillery from New Orleans, captured the original Civil War battle flag of the Ninth Iowa Infantry that was used atop Fort Dubuque with no animosity or disrespect shown toward each other.[218] The Grand Army of the Republic's Joseph A. Mower Post commander from New Orleans messaged the commander of Dubuque's Hyde Clark Post after reading about the encampment and the Washington Artillery in the local newspapers: "Joseph A. Mower Post sends thanks for your kind treatment of our 'Johnny Rebs.'—J.E. Bissell, Commander." General E. Kirby Smith echoed those sentiments.[219]

In his report on the National Military Encampment to the adjutant general of the U.S. Army, Captain William H. Powell remarked, "In the report of my visit to the encampment of the Iowa National Guard last year, I expressed the belief that by encamping a portion of the regular troops with the national guard each year, beneficial results would follow. My expressed belief has been fully realized at this encampment." Due to the success of the Dubuque encampment, greater efforts began in earnest to standardize and share information, techniques and technology between the regular army and the states' national guards through joint training.[220]

One of the recommendations Captain Powell made coming out of the Dubuque encampment was the adoption of the rubber overcoat with sleeves as part of approved army clothing. Captain Powell had seen Iowa National Guard units wearing rubber raincoats the year prior at the Iowa National Guard encampment, where it rained. Captain Powell saw them again in action during his rain-filled week at the encampment in Dubuque. In Powell's report to the adjutant general, he stated:

> *In rainy weather, the overcoat is too heavy for summer, and the poncho too ungainly in appearance, and does not fully protect the soldier, particularly in driving rains, while the rubber coat with sleeves is not only uniform in appearance but enables the soldier to handle his piece with ease. In addition to this, a very serviceable black rubber helmet is manufactured and sold at the low price of 35 cents, which, added to the coat, to take place of the poncho, would make the uniform complete.*[221]

After the encampment ended on June 21, the temporary structures erected for Camp Henderson were taken down, the wood repurposed and the city fairgrounds returned to normal. The city would return to regular daily life once its twenty-thousand-plus visitors had left. All that would remain were the trophies won in competitive drilling and memories of the participants and witnesses. And over the course of several decades, they, too, would be lost to time.

Postscript

The memories of this encampment were lost until March 2017, when this author did a simple search on eBay for all things "Dubuque." One of the many auction listings that appeared was for an "1884 CIVIL WAR TROPHY BUSCH ZOUAVES 8TH MISSOURI INFANTRY PRESENTATION PITCHER." The item's description went on to read, "This is a scarce Civil War Busch Zouaves (8th Missouri Volunteer Infantry 1861–1865) 1884 huge trophy presentation water pitcher." The description listed all the major engagements during the Civil War the Eighth Missouri had fought in and concluded with the inscription found on the pitcher: "First Premium won by the Busch Zouaves Dubuque, Iowa, June 16, 1884."

Left: Silver pitcher first-place prize for Zouave competitive drill at the National Encampment, Dubuque, 1884. *Author's collection.*

Right: Silver pitcher prize inscribed with "First Premium won by the Busch Zouaves at Dubuque, Iowa, June 16th, 1884." *Author's collection.*

As a historian and researcher, this author immediately knew upon reading the inscription that the pitcher was unrelated to the Civil War. Being familiar with Camp Henderson and the 1884 encampment, he assumed this must have been a trophy for an event that was held at the encampment. He won the eBay auction, and the pitcher from the "unique ice-water set of silver" has since returned home to where its story began—Dubuque, Iowa—and where its story may be told once again.

In following up with the seller, this author asked if he knew what happened to the accompanying goblets that went with the pitcher, making it a set. He also asked if the seller knew any of this wonderful piece's history or provenance. The seller only knew for sure what he had read on the inscription. He said the pitcher and stand were in a box that was filled with other unrelated items and stacked among other boxes in an abandoned storage locker he had purchased at auction in Oklahoma, the goblets nowhere to be found. The seller knew nothing more.[222]

Upon further investigation, this author learned that the ice-water pitcher and goblet set were procured for the encampment from A.R. Knight and Co. It was described in the *Dubuque Herald* newspaper as a "tilting pitcher and goblets, in repose or raised work, with a magnificent base."[223] The ice pitcher set was on display in the A.R. Knights and Co. store front window the week of the encampment. A.R. Knights and Co., a wholesale jeweler specializing in diamonds and silverware, was owned and operated by Alonzo R. Knights of Dubuque. Knights's store occupied the storefront from 708 to 714 Main Street in Dubuque.[224]

It was also learned that the Busch Zouaves of St. Louis were invited to the encampment and hosted by the Brewers' Association of Dubuque. The unit took its name in honor of the famous St. Louis brewer Adolphus Busch, who, in return, liked to promote the unit as a means of promoting himself.[225] During the week of the encampment, Busch left for Germany to make plans to tour the continent in 1886 with the Busch Zouaves to show off their superior military drilling techniques, including the lightning riffle drill conducted by Sergeants English and Gleason at Dubuque's Opera House the week of the encampment.[226]

With this author's rediscovery of the ice-water pitcher, he concluded upon learning its history that the best way to honor its memory was to tell the story of its journey. So, the memories of the sham battle and the trophies valiantly won on the drilling fields of Camp Henderson long ago—once lost to time—are rediscovered and told here once again.

WILLIAM BOYD ALLISON

Father of the U.S. Senate

Everyone across America knew his name and the measure of his character at the turn of the twentieth century. Twelve years after his death in 1908, the richest man in the world, Scottish steel baron Andrew Carnegie, described his forty-year friendship with the sage from Dubuque as "a lifelong, unbroken friendship with one of America's best and most valuable public men."[227]

William Boyd Allison was a frontier lawyer, banker and railroad man during the middle-nineteenth century who rose to become the "father of the Senate" and the "Nestor of Republicanism" by the turn of the twentieth century. A radical progressive Republican turned conservative, Allison provided counsel and friendship to every United States president from Abraham Lincoln to Theodore Roosevelt from his seat on the hill in the U.S. Congress and from his home of fifty-plus years at 1134 Locust Street in Dubuque, Iowa.

William Boyd Allison was, once upon a time, a well-known actor on the stage of American history who played minor and major roles in the decisions that shaped the growth and development of modern-day America. Today, Allison has been mostly forgotten by history and relegated to its footnotes.

Few historians, let alone your average American, know the name of William Boyd Allison, a onetime giant of the U.S. Senate and perennial contender for the Republican nomination for president of the United States. Even fewer know how close this forgotten U.S. Senator came to becoming the twenty-sixth president, even though his name never appeared before voters on a presidential ballot. Had he decided differently in 1900, the legacy of President William Boyd Allison and not Theodore Roosevelt would be scribed on the official parchments of U.S. history.

EARLY YEARS

William Boyd Allison was born to John and Margaret Allison on their Wayne County, Ohio farm near Perry on March 2, 1829.[228] After being educated at Wooster Academy in Wayne County, Ohio, and Allegheny College in Pennsylvania, the young William graduated from Western Reserve College in Hudson, Ohio. Allison then turned to the study of law in the office of Hemphill and Turner in Wooster, Ohio. Allison then moved to Ashland, Ohio, to begin practicing law after passing the state bar in 1851. Soon after establishing his law practice, Allison met and fell in love with Anna Carter. The young couple was married in 1854.[229]

Allison started out his political career as a delegate and convention secretary at the Ohio state Republican convention in 1855. It was a role Allison would play at the Republican National Convention of 1860 for his newly adopted state of Iowa after the Buckeye took flight and became a Hawkeye in April 1857, when he and his wife Anna followed his brother Matthew to live in the burgeoning Key City to the Northwest—Dubuque, Iowa.[230]

Allison obtained his interest in politics from his father, an old-school Whig, and started to become politically ambitious during the 1852 presidential campaign for "Old Fuss and Feathers," Winfield Scott. Around this time, Allison first met a young John Sherman, who came to Ashland, Ohio, to give a political speech.[231] Allison would go on to become a warm lifelong friend with the future U.S. senator, U.S. secretary of the treasury, U.S. secretary of state and younger brother of Civil War hero William Tecumseh Sherman.

Allison continued to pursue his interest in Republican Party politics when he settled with his wife in Dubuque. In 1859, Allison was named as a delegate to the Iowa state Republican convention in Des Moines, where he worked to get his fellow former Ohioan Samuel Kirkwood elected governor of Iowa. During the state convention, the ambitious Allison was elected as a delegate to the Republican National Convention, which was to be held in Chicago in May 1860.

After moving to Dubuque, Allison joined Benjamin M. Samuels and Dennis N. Cooley in the law firm of Samuels, Cooley and Allison. Benjamin

Samuels was a Dubuque Democrat and onetime law partner of William Vandever, who lost the 1860 Iowa Second Congressional District House election to the incumbent Vandever.[232] Dennis N. Cooley was a Dubuque Republican who was the secretary of the National Republican Congressional Committee during President Lincoln's reelection campaign in 1864 and was appointed land commissioner of South Carolina by President Lincoln that same year. In 1865, President Andrew Johnson appointed Cooley commissioner of Indian affairs.[233]

Allison would experience two impressionable events in 1860 that would stay with him the rest of his life. The first was the passing of his beloved wife, Anna, in their newly adopted home of Dubuque. Anna's unexpected death from "pulmonary disease" threw Allison into a depression, and he threw himself into his work and Republican politics.[234] The second event was the now-famous 1860 Republican National Convention in Chicago that nominated Abraham Lincoln for president of the United States and Allison's insignificant, if not interesting, role in bringing forth the greatest president our nation has ever known.[235]

Nominating Lincoln

The 1860 convention was held in a packed Wigwam convention center in Chicago, Illinois. Arriving as a state delegate from Iowa, Allison was soon elected assistant convention secretary for the state of Iowa and was seated in front of the desk of convention president George Ashmun of Massachusetts.

Allison did not initially cast his one-fourth of one vote for Lincoln at the convention; he instead first voted for fellow Ohioan Salmon P. Chase. Allison was familiar with Chase's views from the 1855 Ohio Republican Convention when Senator Chase was nominated for Ohio governor. Allison did come around to voting for Lincoln on the third ballot of the contentious convention and was the first of the convention secretaries to tabulate the third ballot votes and announce to the convention president George Ashmun that Abraham Lincoln had received the necessary number of votes to become the Republican Party's nominee for president of the United States.[236]

Samuel Kirkwood won the Iowa gubernatorial election of 1859, and Abraham Lincoln won the presidential election of 1860, and Iowa Republicans from the Mississippi River to the Missouri River were anxious and excited for what the future might bring with Republicans in the state and federal executive mansions. A contingent of young Republicans from

Dubuque and other cities across Iowa, including William Boyd Allison and Grenville Dodge, a young railroad engineer from Council Bluffs, Iowa, made the journey eastward to the capital city of Washington, D.C., to see Abraham Lincoln take the solemn oath prescribed by the Constitution of the United States.

This was not the first time the two young Republicans had seen Lincoln. In 1908, James Morrow of the *Washington Post* ask Senator Allison, who was by then the longest-serving U.S. congressman in history, whether he had ever seen Lincoln. "Many times. I saw him in Dubuque in 1859," proclaimed the Nestor of Republicanism. "I distinctly recollect that he traveled in a private car, being at the time an attorney for the Illinois Central Railroad."[237]

Morrow asked Senator Allison how Lincoln looked at the time. "Pretty gaunt," Allison recalled:

> But he was already a famous man in the West because of his talents as a lawyer and his activity as a Republican. When I heard he was in town, I went to the hotel to see him. However, I didn't feel important enough to make his acquaintance. I next saw him when he was inaugurated as president, coming to Washington with a party of ardent young Republicans, among whom was Grenville M. Dodge, later a major general in the army, chief engineer of the Union Pacific Railroad and a banker.[238]

Dodge had personally met with Lincoln in Council Bluffs, Iowa, in August 1859, one month after Allison saw Lincoln at the Julien House in Dubuque.

Civil War

With the inauguration of President Lincoln and the outbreak of the Civil War, Allison joined the staff of Governor Kirkwood as an aid and was given the rank of lieutenant colonel in the Iowa militia and commissioned to raise men, money and munitions to help Iowa fill its portion of President Lincoln's call for seventy-five thousand troops to turn down the rebellion. Lieutenant Colonel Allison helped raise four Iowa regiments and thousands in both men and treasure before falling ill in the winter of 1861–62.[239]

It was during the organization of the Twelfth Iowa Infantry in 1861 in Dubuque that Allison met a young student from Upper Iowa University by the name of David Bremner Henderson. Allison encouraged Henderson to go back to Upper Iowa University and organize a company of students.

Henderson did just that, organizing the famed Company C of the Twelfth Iowa Infantry with his brothers. Henderson was shot in the neck during the final charge at Fort Donelson and lost his left foot at the Second Battle of Corinth during the first half of the war while fighting with the Twelfth Iowa. After recovering from the loss of his left foot, Henderson reenlisted in the Forty-Sixth Iowa Infantry and served until the end of the war, mustering out as a colonel. Henderson would experience a succession of amputations to his left leg over the remainder of his life, and the wound eventually claimed his entire leg up to the hip. Henderson would go on to be elected to Allison's old Iowa congressional seat in the U.S. House in 1882 and would rise to that body's speakership in 1899.[240]

ELECTION OF 1862

With the census of 1860 came redistricting in Iowa and the state's expansion from two congressional districts to six in 1862. Dubuque was in the Second Congressional District of Iowa since the state's inception and was being represented at the time by Allison's fellow Dubuque Republican William Vandever. With redistricting, Dubuque was to become a part of the newly created Third Congressional District.[241] Congressman Vandever, who had also been serving as the colonel of the Ninth Iowa Infantry since September 24, 1861, and was undergoing a congressional investigation into his dual service, decided not to run for a third term in the U.S. Congress, choosing instead to remain in the Union army for the duration of the war.

Lieutenant Colonel Allison had been working feverishly since the start of the war to recruit, equip and muster soldiers into the Iowa militia in Dubuque while fighting a local war with the "traitors" and "secessionist" newspaper editors of the *Dubuque Daily Herald*, who were openly discouraging enlistment in the Iowa militia and Union army. The *Dubuque Daily Herald* was a Democratic newspaper run by two hardline Stephan A. Douglas Democrats, Dennis Mahony and Stilson Hutchins, who opposed the Lincoln administration and the war against the South.[242]

Mahony was arrested by the Lincoln administration on August 14, 1862, at his home in Dubuque for "discouraging enlistments" through his newspaper and was held without charge or trial in the Old Capital Prison in Washington, D.C., for three months.[243] Upon surrendering to U.S. marshall Herbert "Hub" Hoxie and his posse in Dubuque, Mahony dramatically proclaimed for all his neighbors listening, "Here I am, a martyr for liberty."[244]

Stilson Hutchins joined Mahony at the *Daily Herald* in 1862. Hutchins came to Dubuque from Des Moines, where he had been the owner-editor of the *Iowa State Journal*. Stilson Hutchins is most notable for being the founding owner-editor of the *Washington Post* (1877 to 1889).[245]

After Mahony's arrest and imprisonment, Hutchins became the sole owner and editor of the paper and changed its name to the *Dubuque Democratic Herald*.[246] Mahony, Hutchins and a minority partner in the *Dubuque Daily Herald*, John Hodnett, would reunite to start the *St. Louis Times* immediately after the Civil War in 1866.[247]

Allison was nominated by his fellow Iowa Republicans over Dubuquer Shubael Pratt Adams for U.S. representative from the newly created Third Congressional District on August 6, 1862.

Shubael P. Adams's son John Taylor Adams, born in Dubuque in 1862, was Allison's last campaign manager, helping Allison capture his seventh and final nomination for the U.S. Senate in 1908. Allison died before the Iowa legislature could vote to turn his nomination into a seventh term.[248]

Mahony, Hutchins and the *Herald* denounced Allison as a Republican abolitionist, claiming, "As a neighbor and fellow citizen, we respect Mr. Allison, but as a politician, we look upon him as one of those who have brought our country to its perilous condition, and now still persist in their evil ways making the evil they have done already worse day by day." Mahony and Hutchins predicted that Allison and the Republicans would be beat by whomever the Democracy, as the Democrats were commonly referred to at the time, nominated later in the month. The *Herald* suggested that the only way the Republicans could win was through bribery, deceit and the promise of "government contracts, free passes over the railroads, in the stagecoaches, set on steamboats, all of which will be brought into requisition without stint or limit to secure the election of the abolition Republican candidate."[249]

Even though Mahony sat in a federal prison in Washington, D.C., on August 20, 1862, the Iowa Third District Democratic Convention nominated him, one of the recognized leaders of the Iowa Democratic movement and the most vocal state Democrat opposed to the Lincoln administration, in a divided convention.[250]

Stilson Hutchins was an active participant in getting his business partner and fellow Democrat Mahony nominated, but he failed to get the convention to make the nomination unanimous. Mahony won the nomination fifty-two two-thirds votes to his opponent's fifty-one one-third votes. Several district Democratic newspapers, including the *West Union Pioneer*, refused to endorse Mahony and demanded his nomination's withdrawal.[251]

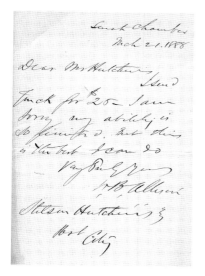

A letter from Senator Allison to Stilson Hutchins, who was raising money for the purchase of a home for the widow of General Winfield Scott Hancock, March 21, 1888. *Author's collection.*

The *Burlington Daily Hawk Eye Gazette* chastised Hutchins, who was then the senior editor of the *Dubuque Daily Herald*, for not understanding why loyal Union Democrats of the district did not fully support Mahony's nomination by exalting, "You have done good work, however, Stilson, in nominating Mahony. You have drawn the line between patriot and traitors, and persuade, scold and bluster as much as you please, you cannot obliterate it."[252]

On October 14, 1862, the Republican abolitionist William Boyd Allison beat the Democratic prisoner of state Dennis A. Mahony 12,112 votes to 8,452 for the right to join the Thirty-Eighth Congress of the United States.[253]

Allison's victory was due in part to Mahony's Copperhead antiwar/pro-South stance, but it was also due to a new and pioneering law in Iowa that was ushered through by Governor Kirkwood and the state legislature. The law allowed soldiers in the field to vote in the 1862 election through a military absentee ballot system.[254] It is yet to be discovered the extent to which Allison and Kirkwood's 1862 election maneuver allowing soldiers to vote from the field was employed as a national tactical strategy by those working feverishly to get President Lincoln reelected at the peak of the Civil War in 1864. It is highly probable that Allison's former Dubuque law partner and secretary for the 1864 Republican Congressional Committee to Re-elect the President, Dennis N. Cooley, learned from what he saw at home in the 1862 midterm election of Allison and employed a similar national strategy, encouraging Union soldier voting from the warfront in states' elections.[255]

Representative William Boyd Allison entered the U.S. Congress on March 4, 1863, starting a career that would end with him being the longest-serving congressman in U.S. history at the time of his death, with 43 years and 152 days of service in Congress. Today, Allison is ranked twenty-third overall in terms of years in service; he is 15 years and 234 days behind the most-tenured member, retired representative John Dingell (D-MI).[256]

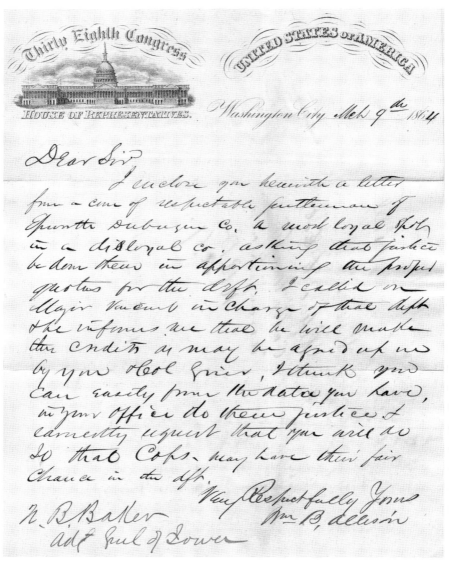

A letter from Representative Allison to Adjunct General Baker regarding Epworth, Dubuque County, being a "most loyal spot in a disloyal county," March 9, 1864. *Author's collection.*

Allison's freshman congressional class of 1863 included two other Republican stalwarts of the second half of the nineteenth century, James A. Garfield and James A. Blaine.

Representative Allison was assigned to the Committees on Public Lands and Roads and Canals in the Thirty-Eighth Congress.[257] During his first term in Congress, Allison promoted the westward expansion of railroads in Iowa as American companies raced to be the first to build a transcontinental railroad. Allison used his private sector banking experience to focus on funding the war effort while demonstrating a keenness for congressional financing and debt management, earning the young congressman a seat on the powerful House Ways and Means Committee in the Thirty-Ninth Congress.[258]

Allison served four terms as the U.S. representative from Iowa's Third District before stepping aside for a fifth term to run for the U.S. Senate seat formerly held by James Grimes. Grimes was the legal guardian of Mrs. Grimes's niece and Allison's future wife, Mary Nealley. Senator Grimes is considered the father of the U.S. Congressional Medal of Honor, introducing legislation in 1861 to establish the prestigious honor for American war heroes.[259]

Grimes resigned his Senate seat in 1869 due to failing health and the uproar over his Senate vote saving President Johnson from being convicted during his Senate impeachment trial. Grimes was replaced by James B. Howell, who served out the remaining thirteen months of Grimes's term. Allison lost to George G. Wright in the 1870 contest to fill the next six-year term of the Iowa Class 2 U.S. Senate seat.

FORESHADOWING NATIONAL SCANDALS

Allison did not return to the Forty-Second U.S. Congress, having chosen not to run for reelection for his Third District House seat while also losing his bid for Iowa's U.S. Senate seat that was once held by the Honorable James Grimes.

Allison's prior two elections in 1866 and 1868 foretold of the gathering storm clouds on the national political horizon. Graft, greed and unchecked power were fuels that drove the Gilded Age coming out of the Civil War. Many of these abuses would come out of the shadows and into the spotlight during the Grant administration. Historians unfairly attribute many of the scandals to an ineptness on the part of General Grant when many of the scandals started or occurred before Grant was president or included no involvement from the president.

Two such scandals touched Congressman Allison in his reelection bids in 1866 and 1868, with their foundation rooted in legislation passed by Representative Allison and the U.S. Congress in 1864. The Whiskey Ring tax scandal grew out of the 1864 Internal Revenue Act, while the Crédit Mobilier railroad scandal sprouted from the Pacific Railroad Acts amendment of 1864.

The Internal Revenue Act of June 30, 1864, placed a large tax on distillers of whiskeys, high-wines and spirits, starting with $1.50 per gallon in 1865 and $2.00 per gallon in 1866 to help pay back the debt brought on by the Civil War and Reconstruction. This was a significant increase from the $0.20-per-gallon tax in 1863 and the $0.70-per-gallon tax in 1864. The demand and sale of distilled alcohol boomed from 1861 to 1865, with the volume of alcohol produced and sold increasing year after year. Early profits of established distillers drew a wave of new competition and increased supply into the market, eventually depressing prices and profits and creating a surplus in wines, whiskeys and other alcoholic spirits.[260]

In 1863, the national average price per gallon of whiskey was $0.44 to $0.78 per gallon, while the tax was $0.20 per gallon. In 1864, prices ranged from $0.60 to $2.03 per gallon, with taxes at $0.70 per gallon. In 1865, the price per gallon skyrocketed to $1.92 to $2.25 per gallon, with the new tax of $1.50 per gallon taking affect. In 1866, the year the $2.00-per-gallon tax took effect, the average price per gallon for whiskey was $2.00 to $2.33.[261]

When the market soured to the dramatic increase in the price of alcohol due to the jump in taxes, many distillers, both old and new, big and small, looked for creative ways to finance their businesses, move their product and protect their investments. The demand for alcohol was still there and growing. But the desire to pay the tax was not. The consumer and the distiller both looked for ways to accommodate one another, legally or otherwise. So, many distillers, who were responsible for paying the tax, turned to tax evasion.

One such distiller was J.A. Rhomberg and Company of Dubuque, Iowa. Joe Rhomberg, a Dubuque industrialist, invested heavily in a large distillery and brewery along the Seventh Street levee in Dubuque in 1863–64, prior to the passage of the 1864 Internal Revenue Act. By the winter of 1864, Rhomberg was manufacturing a wide variety of wines, whiskeys and other spirits, as well as manufacturing all his own barrels and boxes from raw lumber for shipping his products to the markets in the East.[262]

In early 1865, the Rhomberg distillery had produced and shipped to distributors in Buffalo and New York City over 163,000 gallons of alcohol, paying taxes, or duty, on 79,183 gallons while evading taxes on 83,817 gallons of alcohol. The distributors had made advances on the alcohol in good faith and under the assumption that Rhomberg had paid the required taxes. In one or two instances, distributors and creditors had inquired with tax collectors about whether Rhomberg was in good standing with his taxes. They were told by the government that he was.[263]

E.A. Rollins, the commissioner of internal revenue, wrote to Secretary of the Treasury Hugh McCullough in January 1866, explaining that in early April 1865, revenue collector Dorsheimer and tax assessor Presbrey of the Thirteenth District of New York were alerted to large volumes of distilled spirits passing through Buffalo under suspicious circumstances.[264]

In their investigation, Dorsheimer and Presbrey discovered the alcohol was being shipped to three distributors in Buffalo and New York City from the J.A. Rhomberg and Co. distillery in Dubuque, Iowa. When auditing shipments and quantities seized in distributor warehouses and comparing them to railroad shipping records and the tax logs, it became clear that J.A Rhomberg and Co. was evading taxes. Upon the seizure of all the shipped alcohol found in New York State and the seizure of all the properties of J.A. Rhomberg and Co. in Dubuque by the Treasury Department, Joe Rhomberg secured financing from two banks to pay the taxes due on the seized alcohol in an effort to free it to be able to sell it to use the money to help fund the payment for the evaded taxes.[265]

The Dubuque branch of the State Bank of Iowa, commonly known as the Dubuque Branch Bank, advanced Rhomberg roughly $158,000, and the banking firm of Sturges and Company of Chicago advanced Rhomberg approximately $262,000 to procure bonds against the taxes due. Representative Allison, who was a director and had a financial interest in the Dubuque Branch Bank, was asked by the president of the State Bank of Iowa Mr. Randall to speak to the secretary of the treasury about accepting the bonds for taxes due to expedite the process of getting the seized alcohol and property released so it could be sold (and help pay the back taxes) before the product spoiled. Allison happily agreed to do this.[266]

The *Dubuque Daily Herald*, a Democratic newspaper that often lacked scruples in its effort to tell the truth, wove a tale of fraud on the part of Allison, accusing him of being a paid attorney for the government prosecution while also being a defendant in the case as a paid director of the Dubuque Branch Bank who inappropriately imposed on the case with the secretary of the treasury in his capacity as a U.S. representative, causing a loss to the U.S. government of hundreds of thousands of dollars of back taxes and penalty fees the government could have realized had it not been for the fraudulent activities of Representative Allison, as alleged by the *Herald*.[267]

The *Dubuque Daily Herald*'s accusations fell on deaf ears, both within the government's group of investigators and among Iowa voters, as Allison was reelected in 1866 and again in 1868. It is clear after a closer examination of the allegations by the *Herald* that Allison was not engaged in any fraudulent or unscrupulous activities. It is also clear through statements made by the secretary of the treasury and the revenue commissioners that Representative Allison did not try to influence the case one way or another.[268]

The J.A. Rhomberg and Co. case became the first of a long list of whiskey tax fraud cases that would come before the Department of the Treasury after 1864, and it would ultimately lead to the Whiskey Ring scandal and investigation by the Treasury Department during the Grant administration in 1875 and 1876.[269]

The St. Louis Whiskey Ring fraud of 1871–75, which was investigated by the Treasury Department in 1875–76, was a broad conspiracy by Republican Party officials, distillers, local tax collectors and the personal secretary of the president of the United States to divert whiskey tax revenue from the national coffers into Republican campaign accounts and, eventually, into individuals' personal pockets.

The particulars of the scandal did not mirror those of the "whiskey ring fraud" perpetrated by J.A. Rhomberg and Co. Nor was Allison involved or investigated by Congress as part of this scandal. However, one of Allison's friends and a former intern who studied law in Allison's law offices in Dubuque in 1866 was one of the leading characters in this scandal that grabbed the nation's attention.

The scandal revolved around a scheme to syphon whiskey tax revenues, which were on the rise due to the government's crackdown on tax evasion, starting with the Rhomberg case, into local Republican Party accounts that were then used to help fund campaigns and support Republican initiatives. The epicenter of the scandal was the Missouri District in St. Louis and revenue collector and former Union general John McDonald. McDonald was working with the local revenue agent for the district Colonel John A. Joyce.

The two-year investigation and prosecution resulted in the indictment of three individuals: John McDonald, John A. Joyce and President Grant's personal secretary, Orville Babcock, who was also involved in the fraud.

McDonald and Joyce were convicted of their charges and served time in a federal penitentiary. Orville Babcock was acquitted of all charges thanks to a trial deposition given by President Grant in which the president exonerated Babcock solely on his personal belief that Babcock would never do such a thing. The president was sadly mistaken and clearly impacted justice as it related to Orville Babcock.[270]

John A. Joyce grew up in Mount Sterling, Kentucky, and moved to Allamakee County, Iowa, after leaving the Twenty-Fourth Kentucky Infantry, a pro-Union regiment, in early 1865. After working a stint as an Iowa tax collector and a run for the Iowa state legislature in the summer and fall of 1865, Joyce found himself studying law in the office of Allison, Crane and Rood in Dubuque, where he received his license to practice law in November 1866. Joyce then moved to Washington, D.C., where fate and Representative Allison intervened to secure Joyce a position with the commissioner of internal revenue in Missouri.[271]

After serving time for his involvement in the "St. Louis Whiskey Ring," Joyce went on to become a regular contributor to the *Washington Post* and a poet laureate for the Civil War veteran. Joyce is one of two authors who lay claim to the poem "Love and Laughter" (also known as "Solitude"), which starts out, "Laugh, and the world laughs with you, weep, and you weep alone."[272]

Today, the poem is generally attributed to Ella Wheeler Wilcox, but for nearly fifty years, the authorship was in dispute and was attributed to "anonymous." Wilcox had the first publication of the poem that can be verified, published in 1883; however, during the decades-long public dispute between Joyce and Wilcox over the poem's authorship, Joyce had numerous witnesses come forward and validate his version of the story—where it does not appear Mrs. Wilcox did.

In 1899, during one of the pair's public spats in the newspapers over the authorship of the poem, the *St. Louis Post-Dispatch* published several reader letters regarding the Wilcox-Joyce controversy. Most of the letter writers indicated that they remember learning the poem as a child in the 1860s in either Illinois

Representative Allison's law firm intern John A. Joyce. *Photographer, S.J. Lovewell, Dubuque, 1866; author's collection.*

or Kentucky or scrapbooking the poem from the local newspaper.[273] Joyce claimed he wrote the poem for the editor of the *Louisville Journal*, who published it in 1863. The former secretary to the editor of the *Journal* stated in a letter to Joyce, published in the *Louisville Courier-Journal*, that she remembered a similar poem being printed in the *Journal* during the war.[274]

Regardless, Americans became weary of hearing about the controversy every few years, and cynical editors took their shots in the national newspapers. The *New Orleans Times-Picayune* wryly stated, "Upon a compromise basis, it has been decided that 'Laugh and the world laughs with you,' was written by Ella John Wheeler Wilcox Joyce."[275] The *El Paso Herald*, regarding the "tiresome quarrel," suggested one way to end the controversy in 1902: "Why don't they get married, and then it will all be in the family."[276]

From 1868 to 1872, Allison was focused on two primary interests: railroads and the U.S. Senate. Allison had a desire to be back in Congress and fancied himself a United States senator, so he set his sights on the 1872 election and Iowa's Class 3 U.S. Senate seat held by James Harlan.

In the meantime, Allison's second area of focus was one he had built his legal career around—railroads. Allison was a director of the Dubuque and Sioux City Railroad, elected in 1867, and he and his law partner George Crane were the legal counsel for the Illinois Central Railroad in Dubuque for nearly a decade.[277] Congressman Allison was also the president of the Dunleith and Dubuque Bridge Company, which built the fifth railroad bridge across the Mississippi River in 1868, connecting the Illinois Central Railroad with the Dubuque and Sioux City Railroad between Dunleith (present-day East Dubuque), Illinois, and Dubuque, Iowa.[278]

In the winter of 1868, a young man from Pittsburgh, Pennsylvania, came to Dubuque to convince Allison and the board of directors of the Dunleith and Dubuque Bridge Co. to award the contract for the building of its bridge to his company. So started the forty-year friendship between Andrew Carnegie of the Keystone Bridge Works Co. and William Boyd Allison of the Key City to the Northwest.[279]

Carnegie would describe the undertaking in his autobiography: "We were competing for the building of the most important railway bridge that had been built up to that time, a bridge across the wide Mississippi at Dubuque, to span which was considered a great undertaking," professed the great American industrialist.[280]

Allison and the Dunleith and Dubuque Bridge Co. hired engineer Roswell B. Mason to oversee the construction of its span over the Mississippi River in August 1867. In the 1850s, Mason was the chief engineer who oversaw

The Dunleith and Dubuque Bridge Co. stock shares issued to Senator Allison on December 28, 1874. *Author's collection.*

the construction of the 705-mile-long Illinois Central Railroad and the first 21 miles of the Dubuque and Pacific Railroad, which became the Dubuque and Sioux City Railroad in 1860. Mason moved to Chicago after completing the bridge in Dubuque and was elected mayor of the Windy City in time to preside over the Great Chicago Fire of 1872.[281]

During the presidential election of 1872, a railroad scandal was brewing in the national newspapers that was about to blow the dome off the U.S. Capitol. Congressman Oakes Ames, a Republican businessman from Easton, Massachusetts, and the namesake of Ames, Iowa, was being accused of giving or selling stock to other congressmen at a discounted rate for special consideration related to the construction of the Union Pacific Railroad and its construction company, the Crédit Mobilier Company of America.[282]

Oakes Ames was a leading investor and the vice-president of the Central Pacific Railroad Company, which, along with the Union Pacific Railroad Company, created the first transcontinental railroad across America. Toward the end of the American Civil War in 1865, President Lincoln asked Representative Ames to take control of the troubled construction company that was building the Union Pacific Railroad—Crédit Mobilier—and get the line completed and opened from sea to shining sea.[283]

Among those caught up in the fermenting scandal were outgoing vice president Schuyler Colfax, then-current candidate and next vice president Henry Wilson, future president James Garfield and four Iowans: former congressman, Allison's friend and chief engineer of the Union Pacific Railroad Grenville Dodge; former U.S senator James Grimes; current U.S. senator James F. Wilson; and newly elected U.S. senator William Boyd Allison.[284]

Both Ames and Allison had business interests in the many railroads that were being built crisscrossing Iowa in the 1860s as the nation raced to complete the first transcontinental railroad. In 1864, Ames and Allison were successful in getting funding for the creation of a federally backed railroad, the Sioux City and Pacific Railroad, into the Pacific Railroad Acts amendment of 1864, which was signed by President Lincoln. Representative Allison had directly asked President Lincoln to designate the railroad a federal land grant railroad, opening it up to federal bond financing and federal land grants.[285] Lincoln approved. The Sioux City and Pacific Railroad corporate offices were originally based in Dubuque, with railroad baron John I. Blair as its president and Congressmen Oakes Ames and William B. Allison as corporate directors.[286]

Allison was offered stock in Crédit Mobilier and the Union Pacific Railroad by Ames while both men served in the U.S. House in 1868. Allison became uneasy about the transaction after the initial offer by Ames and returned the stock and a round of dividends sent by Ames in 1868.[287]

Ames initially testified before a House committee investigating the matter that Representative Allison had purchased ten shares of stock in Crédit Mobilier.[288] Allison immediately responded to the committee, defending himself in writing and calling into question Mr. Ames's memory:

> *Please say to your committee that Oakes Ames is in error. He mailed to me ten shares of Union Pacific and ten shares of Crédit Mobilier certificates. I returned the certificates to him by mail. He also sent me a check for one Mobilier dividend, to which I had no claim. I included the amount of the check in a sight draft on New York, payable to his order. Please disclaim, on my behalf, any share holding an interest in the Crédit Mobilier, or Union Pacific stocks. I have not had any, I have not derived any profit therefrom. Wm B. Allison.[289]*

Oakes Ames later validated that Allison had sent his stock certificates and a draft check for the dividend back to him, while Ames's and Allison's

Left: William Boyd Allison, U.S. representative, Iowa, circa 1863. *Right*: Oakes Ames, U.S. representative, Massachusetts, circa 1863. *Photographer, Mathew Brady; Library of Congress.*

finer details of the transaction seem to differ. Ames thought Allison foresaw a difficult election ahead in Iowa and did not want the appearance of impropriety in owning the stock, so he returned it.[290]

Oakes Ames was censured by the House of Representatives in February 1873 for "seeking to procure congressional attention to the affairs of a corporation in which he was interested."[291] Allision emerged from the scandal unscathed, removing himself from all his active business interests to focus on his senatorial career for the next thirty-plus years.[292]

Entering the Senate

Allison had lost his first bid to become a United States senator against George Wright in 1870, having declined to run for reelection for his seat in the U.S. House in the hopes of filling the seat vacated by Senator James Grimes. Allison spent the next two years planning to unseat his fellow Republican, incumbent U.S. senator James Harlan.

Harlan was more of a conservative Republican, whereas Allison was still a radical, or progressive, Republican going back to his days in the House in the 1860s.

The Iowa legislature surprised the Washington elite and many throughout Iowa when it upset Harlan and selected Allison to be the next U.S. senator from the Hawkeye State.

Senator Allison's first order of business was to get beyond the Crédit Mobilier scandal, which he was successful in doing.

In 1874, Senator Allison was named the chairman of the Congressional Joint Select Committee to Inquire into the Affairs of the District of Columbia, also known as the Allison Committee. Up to this point, the city of Washington, D.C., was administered by a governor appointed by the U.S. Congress and was bursting with debt from alleged mismanagement.

The Allison Committee did not hold back in shining the spotlight on all the problems within the administration of the District of Columbia under Governor Alexander Shepherd. Allison's committee identified issues in a Congress-appointed governor arbitrarily running the District on behalf of Congress and proposed a "commission" to run the municipal government that made up one aspect of the nation's capital city. Allison and his committee assumed their plan for a commission to run the municipal government of the City of Washington would be temporary—until a new form of municipal government could be adopted for the District inhabitants that spread responsibility and oversight to multiple officials and not a single arbitrary governor.[293]

The Allison Committee's "Commission Plan" became the standard form of municipal governance for Washington, D.C., and predates the Galveston Plan of 1901 by a quarter century. The commission form of municipal government, along with mayor-council and council-manager make up the three basic forms of municipal governments today.[294]

GREAT SIOUX WAR

In 1874, Lieutenant Colonel George Armstrong Custer verified the discovery of gold in the Black Hills of the Dakota Territory during an exploratory ride into Indian Territory with the Seventh U.S. Cavalry. With the report in the national newspapers, a wave of intrepid White explorers swept across the plains to invade sacred Sioux lands that were guaranteed to the Sioux through the Fort Laramie Treaty of 1868.

It was understood that the first wave of White pioneers would soon turn into a tsunami of White miners and settlers encroaching on Sioux lands, dreaming of striking it rich as America inched its way westward throughout the nineteenth century. To that end, President Grant established a presidential commission in 1875 to travel to the Dakota Territory to negotiate a license with Sitting Bull, Red Cloud, Spotted Tail and Crazy Horse's people to mine for gold in the Black Hills, promising to leave once it was no longer profitable to remove gold from the hills. If the Sioux would so be inclined, the Great Father desired to purchase the Black Hills and have the Sioux relocate.

Senator Allison, the chair of the Senate Committee on Indian Affairs from 1874 to 1879, was appointed by the president to chair what would be commonly known as the Allison Commission.[295] Allison, along with seven other congressmen, clergy, Indian traders and military representatives made up the commission. In August and September 1875, members of the commission traveled to the Red Cloud and Spotted Tail Agencies in northwestern Nebraska for a grand council to negotiate mining rights in, or the outright sale of, the Black Hills and the Big Horn Valley to its west.[296]

Allison told the Sioux that the United States wanted to "buy of you the right for them [miners] to go to the Black Hills, and mine there, and see what they can find. We will give you a just price for the privilege. When the gold is taken away, the country will still be yours, the same as now." Upon translation, the gathered bands of Sioux and Cheyenne warriors

and chieftains involuntarily thundered with disbelieving howls of laughter.[297] The Sioux knew better.

Allison and the commission offered the 4,500-plus Natives at the Grand Council $400,000 per year to allow White miners and settlers to work the Black Hills until such time as the cost to remove the gold outweighed the profit from the gold—to be determined, of course, by the U.S. government.[298]

A second option was offered: the outright purchase of the Black Hills and the Big Horn country for $6 million, paid over fifteen annual installments.[299] Red Cloud, Red Dog, Little Bear, Lone Horn and other Sioux leaders, recognizing the inevitable, asked for $70 million for the Black Hills and refused to give up their sacred lands in the Big Horn country, where Sitting Bull and Crazy Horse's

Oglala Lakota Sioux chief Red Cloud, Washington, D.C., 1880. *Photographer, John K. Hillers; Library of Congress.*

bands then roamed.[300] Red Dog also insisted the Great Father in Washington ensure that the Sioux Nation be taken care of and fed for the next seven generations. Red Cloud and the others echoed Red Dog's request.[301]

Ultimately, the Allison Commission was unable to come to an agreement with the Sioux leaders. A lack of customary presents for the Natives and limits to the commission's ability to negotiate an agreement inhibited the commission from reaching a deal with the Sioux. Sitting Bull and Crazy Horse did not personally participate in the negotiations with Allison and the commission, as they were "off the reservation."[302]

Allison's 1875 *Report of the Commission Appointed to Treat with the Sioux Indians for the Relinquishment of the Black Hills*, recognizing the reluctancy of the Sioux to strike a deal under the Treaty of 1868, recommended the following to the President and Congress:

> *1st. That Congress shall take the initiative upon the whole subject of our relations with the Sioux, and by law make provision for a thorough system of education for all between the ages of six and sixteen years at a point or points distant from contact with or from the influence of adult Indians, which system shall involve manual-labor and industrial schools, and shall be compulsory.*
>
> *2nd. Protect by law every Indian in the acquisition of private property.*
>
> *3rd. Those bands which now occupy the northwestern part of the state of Nebraska be removed therefrom to some point or points within the permanent reservation.*
>
> *4th. All supplies be issued under the direct supervision of officers of the army.*
>
> *5th. Abolish all the present agencies and reorganize the whole system of officers and agencies for the Sioux Nation.*
>
> *6th. Make known to the Indians that a sufficient amount of force will be used to secure compliance with these salutary provisions made for their benefit, to the end that they may become civilized and self-supporting, if possible.*
>
> *7th. Provide for payment to the Indians of a sum which Congress shall fix as a fair equivalent for the Hills, taking into the account all the circumstances surrounding them, and the value of the Hills to the United States, which sum, so offered or paid, shall become a part of the fund required for the purpose hereinbefore indicated.*[303]

Allison's report went on to state, "The plan here suggested, or some other to be adopted by Congress, should be presented to the Indians as a finality, and with it, they should be told that its rejection will have the effect to arrest all appropriations for their subsistence in the future and all supplies not absolutely required by the Treaty of 1868." Allison cautioned that the Sioux "have claims upon us that cannot be overlooked."[304] Basically, the report recommended telling the Sioux that if they did not accept the nonnegotiable terms, the government would honor the basics of the Treaty of 1868, make right that which has been required under law and cut off all other aid and protection—the Natives would be on their own within the territory defined by the treaty, without government assurances or protection. What they did not state was the fact that it was the intention of the government to stop enforcing Grant's order to the army "to protect the reservation from White intrusion," which it had been attempting to do—although very poorly.[305]

Indian inspector William Vandever was in Cheyenne, Wyoming Territory, and at the Red Cloud and Spotted Tail Agencies in May 1876, trying to bring calm to the gathering storm on the Great Plains. At the heart of the storm were the ill-advised actions of the U.S. Army on the plains. On May 22, 1876, Vandever messaged the commissioner of Indian affairs John Q. Smith, "Situation in regard to Indians to serious that I cannot properly explain in writing. I promised the Indians to present their case. They want peace. I feel it my duty to come to Washington tomorrow afternoon. Stopping a day in Dubuque. Am sorry to be compelled to take this responsibility."[306] Vandever followed with a telegram to secretary of the interior Zachariah Chandler: "Am coming to Washington without orders to present Indian matters. I think it important and for good of the service. Feel it my duty to do so. Will present my resignation on my arrival if you desire. Please see my correspondence with commissioner and inform Senator Allison."[307] Vandever saw the writing on the wall.

In an ultimate culmination of the mismanagement of U.S. policy toward the Sioux—and Cheyenne—due in part to ignoring Vandever's pleas from his visit to the plains in May 1876 or the confidential executive decisions made by the president, secretary of war and secretary of the interior to remove the Sioux, whatever the cost as far as the War Department was concerned, the Great Sioux War of 1876 was highlighted by the Battle of the Little Bighorn and Lieutenant Colonel George Armstrong Custer's insubordinate bravado that caused the death of himself and his Seventh U.S. Cavalry.

A shocked nation responded, as did the July 9, 1876 edition of the *Dubuque Daily Times*, a Republican newspaper that was considered an organ of the

This image of General Custer hung in his Fort Abraham Lincoln, Dakota Territory parlor wall along with a portrait of General Phil Sheridan. *National Park Service.*

leader of the Iowa Republican Party, Senator Allison. The article, simply titled "The Indian War," made several proclamations in its condemnation of Generals Crook and Terry and Lieutenant Colonel Custer's misguided actions on the northern plains.

We are of those who deem it best to look the stern facts and philosophy of the case full in the face, rather than surrender entirely to passion and join in the common hue and cry for revenge, for the utter annihilation of the Indian race. Custer and his little troop of less than 300 men were killed in a battle they themselves sought and began. They had traveled hundreds of miles to make war upon Sitting Bull and his people. The fight occurred on unceded ground and to which the Indian title was as good if not better than that of the whites.[308]

The occupation of the Black Hills by thousands of miners is simply an unwarranted trespass, quite exasperating to the Indians. Would white men submit to such an invasion of their property rights without war?…

But they did not make war; it has been the government that has precipitated war in every instance. There have been Indian depredations, thefts, robberies, and the like—though but few—and a few assassinations of mail carriers and miners, but the latter were lawless trespassers. Sitting

Bull and his band are known as the wild Indians, composed of Sioux and Cheyennes [sic]. *A few hundred of the latter were attacked by Gen. Crook last winter and their village destroyed. This maddened them, and they joined Sitting Bull for better protection....*

While deploring the loss of these men, we find it difficult to condemn the Indians. Had they been whites, their defensive fight would have been approved and their success heralded all over the land as a brilliant achievement, and they held up as heroes in bravely resisting the warlike encroachment upon their village.[309]

The *Times* concluded, "Some of these views are entertained by Hon. W.B. Allison, chairman of the Senate Committee of Indian Affairs. They were set forth and urged in his report of last year as commissioner to treat with the Sioux. They are also shared by General Vandever, general Indian inspector, and were elaborated in his May report."[310]

One week after the Battle of Little Bighorn, President Grant's U.S. Indian inspector, General William Vandever of Dubuque, visited the Red Cloud and Spotted Tail Agencies, where Allison held the grand council one year prior. Based on his assessment of affairs, Vandever published an editorial in the August 6, 1876 edition of the *Dubuque Daily Times*.

How much of Vandever's editorial opinion was shared by Senator Allison is unclear. The Allison Commission's report to Congress might suggest that Allison was indifferent to the removal of the Sioux and Cheyenne from the Black Hills and Big Horn Valley based on its final recommendations. The *Daily Times*'s suggestion that Allison, Vandever and the paper shared some of the same views on the matter is not contrary to Allison doing his due diligence in executing the letter of the law as it related to his commission's failed task while trying to give every consideration to the Sioux under the law. Between Allison's commission report and the *Times*'s articles, it would appear that Allison's opinion and his professional duty were to some degree at conflict. Unfortunately for the annals of history, Allison was not as vocal about his true private opinions as was General Vandever.

Vandever summed up the truth of the matter, which was not popular or widely accepted at the time, which is why Allison was probably more reserved if he indeed shared the same views, as suggested by the *Times*.

Vandever, after returning from the Red Cloud Agency, explained to the *Times* reader why a small group of Natives would not return to their reservations or cede the Black Hills or the Big Horn country in his editorial:

Sitting Bull and other Indians who cling to the unceded territory west of the reservation support themselves without aid from the government. They inhabit a country from which white men are excluded by the Treaty of 1868. Why, then, attempt to drive them from it? If the purpose is to destroy the Indians, it matters little whether we drive them to a barren reservation to be starved or exterminate them by means of the army for refusing to go. The latter mode of disposing of the Indians may have the approval of the army, but it will be found to be immensely expensive and can reflect no credit on the American name….

The government, now without justifiable pretext, sends its army into this country to make war and drive the Indians out of it. Under similar circumstances, what people, savage or civilized, would not fight till the last gasp to repel the invader?…

A feeble attempt was made by the government to protect the Indian lands from the trespass of white men…

Gen. Crook, with a cavalry command, left Fort Laramie sometime about the 1st of March last, and moving by way of Fetterman, went into the country west of the Black Hills, attacked and destroyed an Indian village and then returned in haste to Laramie. This unfortunate and ill-advised expedition inaugurated the war. The Indians prior to this had been peaceable—they now flew to arms…

What act had the Indians committed prior to Gen. Crook's first incursion into their country last March to justify the commencement of hostilities?…

The war office in that reply throws the blame upon the Interior Department by saying that Gen. Crook was first sent into the Sioux country to make war on the request of the secretary of the interior. There is no pretense that the Indians were hostile at that time.

We, a civilized nation, are thereby made accessories to the savage barbarities of a warfare that spares neither age nor sex. The very Indians whom we now employ as our allies to exterminate the Sioux may in their turn become our enemies, when there are no more Sioux to subdue. The army will then be required to subjugate and exterminate its present friends. The American name gains no glory by these wars, but its army finds employment, and while every other branch of the public service is curtailed, this is enlarged…

A valorous but barbaric race are fast disappearing before the advancing wave of civilization, deemed to speedy destruction, because they seek to defend from encroachment the lands which this government pledged its honor to maintain as their exclusive possession.

Vandever finished, "We are the aggressors in this war; the Indians up to the present time have acted chiefly on the defensive."[311] This was very blunt and damning language from a sitting member of the Grant administration and was perfectly accurate. While the Great Sioux War of 1876 would drag on into 1877, Allison turned to the portions of his commission's plan that, as a senator, he could control through legislation.

Allison had introduced Senate Bill No. 590 in the first session of the Forty-Fourth Congress to peaceably negotiate the sale of the Black Hills. Allison hoped to avoid military conflict. After Custer's blunder at Little Bighorn, the bill was killed in committee.[312]

President Grant appointed a new commission to negotiate the relocation of the Sioux to Indian Territory in Oklahoma in August 1876. Bishop Henry Whipple, an Episcopalian bishop of Minnesota, was one of the seven members on the commission chaired by former Bureau of Indian Affairs director George Mannypenny.[313] Bishop Whipple enlisted the aid of other clergy to help plan and institute a program to minister to the Natives humanitarian needs related to food, clothing, shelter, et cetera. Reverend Whipple asked Reverend Charles Seymour of Dubuque's St. John Episcopal Church to accompany his party to the reservations in September and October 1876. Upon hearing of his fellow Dubuquer joining the work of the commission, Allison secured Seymour with official credentials for the excursion to visit the Sioux.[314]

The new commission was able to negotiate a reluctant settlement with the Sioux leaders. Senator Allison introduced Senate Bill No. 1185 on January 26, 1877, to ratify and codify the agreement in Congress. The bill passed, and President Grant signed it on February 28, 1877, allowing citizens of the United States to enter the Black Hills and forcing the Sioux onto reservations in the Missouri River Valley instead of Indian Territory in Oklahoma.[315] So, the next stage in America's misguided and destructive efforts to assimilate the "wild" Natives into "civilized society" commenced.

It was during this phase of American history that Allison made the greatest consequential decision of his legislative career. His inclusion of recommendation number one in the commission report, recommending the creation of a system of compulsory boarding schools for Natives aged six to sixteen years to attend, still has damaging effects today.

Allison subscribed to the theory that Native culture was too different in traditions, beliefs, values and way of life from Western society that they could never successfully convert adult Natives roaming freely on the plains to a traditional European American way of life. Allison, swayed by many of the leading "experts" of the day, falsely believed that a child with an impressionable mind could be culturally converted to an agrarian-Christian sensibility and integrated into American "civilized" society in one or two generations, absent influence from the older generation, without harm.

What is not clear is how much Allison looked at the potential for harm of such a policy or how much he may have supported complete and total separation between Native children and their parents, siblings, grandparents, aunts, uncles and communities, with literally no contact. This was all happening in an age when orphan trains herded children from the East Coast to Iowa farm families in the West and when a "home for the friendless" for unwanted or orphaned children could be found in most growing communities.

Based on his record on issues related to Black race relations, the somewhat cryptic suggestions by the *Dubuque Times* that Allison was for fair, equitable and honest treatment in dealing with Natives and his insistence that the U.S. government must honor its contractual obligations with them, it is fair to say Allison did not fall into the same camp as Generals Cook and Sheridan, Secretary of War Belkamp or Secretary of the Interior Chandler when it came to their shameless support for the inhumane treatment of Natives.

Allison, being only one man with an opinion on Native affairs among many in Washington, D.C., focused on ensuring many of the legitimate complaints by the different Native tribes and agencies were addressed after the Battle of Little Bighorn and the much-needed supplies were provided as they should have been under the Treaty of 1868.

Allison's shortsightedness lay in his lack of understanding the long-term impacts of separating children from their families over multiple generations. Allison did not foresee the extreme and unforgivable individual and institutional abuses implicitly and explicitly perpetrated on Natives in reservation and tribal boarding schools over the next century. Sadly, the negative ramifications of such a plan were probably never considered.

Regardless, it does not alter Allison's role in this sad chapter of our collective American history.

INTEGRATING WEST POINT

William Boyd Allison came to the U.S. Congress as a staunch abolitionist and a radical Republican. Throughout his career, he supported and voted for pro-Black causes, including emancipation, supported by his vote for the Thirteenth Amendment to the U.S. Constitution. He also voted for the Fourteenth and Fifteenth Amendments, which provided, at least in letters, equality under the law and Black male suffrage.

On May 4, 1864, Representative Allison delivered a speech on the floor of the House advocating the full force of the law to implement aggressive reconstruction policies. One of those proposed policies supported by Allison would award southern homesteads that were confiscated during the war to Union veterans in southern states that were known to be in rebellion against the federal government. If passed, the act would be implemented by men like Allison's former law partner Dennis Cooley, the acting Union land commissioner of South Carolina in 1864.[316]

In April 1880, Senator Allison was appalled at the news that a lone Black cadet at the U.S. Military Academy at West Point was found unresponsive, cut up and bleeding in his bed, his hands tied. Cadet Johnson Whittaker received his appointment to West Point in 1876 from South Carolina representative Solomon Hoge.[317] Hoge had nominated the first-ever Black cadet, John W. Smith, to the academy in 1870.[318]

On April 26, 1880, during a debate on a pension bill to add noncommissioned officers of the regular army to the eligible "retired list," Senator Allison introduced an amendment to the legislation that required the president to appoint two cadets of color to West Point annually. The amendment was met with hesitation and outright disdain. Some opposed it because they said they did not wish to increase the number of cadets at the time; others were opposed to forced "association between the two races at West Point or anywhere else." Many prefaced their reasons for objecting by explaining that they had always wished the best for Black Americans and that they had always shown them kindness—"however."[319]

Allison explained that he had proposed the amendment to "secure a legislative declaration that it is our [nation's] public policy that West Point shall be open to the colored people, who are now practically excluded."[320]

Allison argued that his amendment was not legislative discrimination, giving favor to Black people over White people, as some had argued. Rather, there had long been discrimination as a matter of fact against Black Americans, because up until Cadet Whittaker, there had only been two Black cadets in the entire history of West Point, and neither of them had managed to graduate through no fault of their own. It was time to level the parade field at West Point by allowing in cadets of color.[321]

During the debates, which lasted several days, Allison dismissed one alleged reason for opposing the amendment after another. Allison argued that the army needed more officers to fill its ranks and showed the military lists supporting the need for an increased number of graduating cadets.[322] On May 20, 1880, in a win for Jim Crow, the Senate passed the noncommissioned officers' pension act without passing Allison's amendment calling for the annual appointment of cadets of color to West Point.[323]

Senator Allison's lifelong dedication to the proposition that all men are created equal and his willingness to vote in alignment with this belief garnered the admiration, support and respect from Black Americans throughout the nation.

In the 1880s, while getting a haircut in Iowa, Senator Allison met and befriended barber John Sims. Sims was a runaway enslaved person from South Carolina who ended up in Oskaloosa, Iowa. The powerful chairman of the Senate Appropriations Committee invited Sims to the U.S. Capitol to work in the Senate barbershop. Sims would go on to become a preacher at the Universal Church of Holiness in Washington, D.C., while spending forty years as a barber at the Capitol and affectionately becoming known as the "Bishop of the Senate." Sims drew the admiration and respect of men like Charles Dawes, Calvin Coolidge and Warren G. Harding.[324]

The highly respected Booker T. Washington wrote to Senator Allison in April 1896, when talk within the Republican party was of nominating Allison for president. Washington assured Allison, though they had never met, that he, Washington, was doing everything he could to get Allison nominated, reasoning, "I am basing my action on the ground that I consider you a wise, conservative and sincere leader and one who can be depended upon to do the right thing in connection with the interests of the race to which I belong."[325]

Allison was even bestowed one of the highest honors given any individual: having someone who is unrelated name their child after them. In 1902, John and Gabrielle Davis named their son William Boyd Allison Davis, who would later go by Allison Davis. Davis was born into an activist family in Washington, D.C., and would rise to be the first Black American to hold a full-time academic position at a major White university—the University of Chicago. It is likely that Davis's father, John, knew Senator Allison from working for years in the Government Printing Office in Washington.[326]

PRESIDENTIAL CONTENDER

For twenty years, the name William Boyd Allison was in perennial contention for the Republican presidential nomination and was always on the short list for top-level cabinet positions while Republican administrations dominated the executive branch throughout his political lifetime.

Allison's first opportunity to join the executive branch of government came in 1881, when Allison's friend Major General James A. Garfield asked him to join his upcoming cabinet. Allison and Garfield's personal friendship dated to 1863, when they entered the Thirty-Eighth U.S. Congress together as freshman members of the House of Representatives.

Senator Allison did not seek a cabinet position, although he was well qualified and at the top of the list to be president-elect Garfield's secretary of the treasury. Allison and outgoing Secretary of the Treasury John Sherman were viewed as the nation's economists, Allison having served on the House Ways and Means Committee and in his current role on the Senate Finance and Appropriations Committees. Allison was also the force behind the Bland-Allison Act, which "authorized the coinage of the standard silver dollar and to restore its legal-tender charter" in the Forty-Fifth Congress.[327]

Allison urged Garfield to place James F. Wilson, a former Iowa congressman, into the seat of the treasury secretary. Garfield believed he needed someone from the West, someone from Iowa, in his cabinet.[328] The president-elect was also receiving pressure from eastern forces against Allison for treasury. Garfield offered Allison the option to take over the Department of Interior. Allison declined, preferring to stay in the Senate. Garfield continued to press Allison to take the treasury position through inauguration day—but to no avail. Ultimately, President Garfield selected Representative William Windom of Minnesota for secretary of the treasury, and Iowa's former war governor Samuel Kirkwood accepted an offer from Garfield at Allison's request to become secretary of the interior.[329]

On March 5, 1881, President James Garfield presented his list of cabinet nominees to the U.S. Senate, which immediately confirmed the cabinet unanimously. Stories with Washington, D.C., datelines listing the names of the new cabinet members appeared in newspapers around the nation. Absent from the list of new cabinet members was the name William Boyd Allison. Nevertheless, Allison was not absent from many of the newspaper stories.

In one such article, after discussing the new cabinet, the article proceeded to sensationalize "Why Allison refused the Treasury." The article, which was carried in the March 6 edition of the *Dubuque Daily Times*, explained the three-month-long "will he, won't he" mystery regarding the treasury and the final decision by Senator Allison in a single sentence: "Thursday night, the secretaryship of the treasury was formally tendered Senator Allison, and after taking all night to consider it, he declined yesterday because of the ill health of Mrs. Allison, and he feared the social duties that would be imposed upon her might be fatal to her."[330] The *Washington, D.C. Evening Star* explained, "Mrs. Allison is not in the enjoyment of good health and is subject to nervous attacks."[331]

The *Lincoln* (NE) *Journal* poked fun at what they called Allison's "novel excuse," calling it "an excuse that is seldom offered in these degenerate days and it is not likely to be duplicated by anyone unless it be at some future time by Mr. Allison himself." The paper went on to chastise Allison for choosing his wife's health over "honor, riches and all else which a lofty cabinet position would bring."[332]

Mary Nealley Allison, the wife of Senator William Boyd Allison, would try to take her own life sixteen days before President James Garfield passed away on September 19, 1881, from wounds sustained from an assassin's bullet on July 2, 1881. Mrs. Allison tried to drown herself in Silver Lake, near Warsaw, New York, while she was an "inmate of Mrs. Green's water cure in Castile." When asked why she tried to kill herself, Mary Allison rationalized, "I wanted to drown myself and not cause my husband any more trouble."[333] This would not be Mary's last attempt to escape her torment and suffering.

After three years of battling insomnia and "nervous prostration," a condition attributed to anxiety and depression, Mary Allison drowned herself in the Mississippi River in Dubuque near Moore's Mill, in the vicinity of today's Maus Park. While Senator Allison was out stumping in Iowa, Mrs. Allison told members of her household that she was going to go visit Mrs. D.B. Henderson. Instead, Mary went down to the river, waded out into three feet of water, secured rocks in her coat pockets and one in a cloak tied around her neck and laid down in the river in the hopes that the warm, flowing summer waters of Old Man River would wash away her years of pain and anguish.[334]

It is not certain what caused Mary Allison's anxiety and depression. Her first attempt to take her life was most likely exacerbated by all the press she received in the stories around her husband not accepting the secretaryship of the treasury due to her "domestic issues." Her death, however, was not brought on by a singular event or a single sudden urge to end her life. One must wonder if the 19 years and 321 days between the older William and the younger Mary played into her feeling like she was causing her husband trouble.[335]

Senator Allison considered running for president in 1884, when the Republican Party decided not to run President Chester A. Arthur for reelection. Allison declined to run when his friend and fellow freshman from the congressional class of 1863 made it known he would be seeking the Republican nomination. James Blaine would receive the Republican Party's nomination and ended up losing the general election to Democrat Grover Cleveland.

In 1888, the field was wide open to contenders for the Republican presidential nomination, and William B. Allison was interested and well positioned to make a run. Newspapers around Iowa and the nation had Allison as a top-tier contender, along with Senator John Sherman of Ohio, Senator Benjamin Harrison of Indiana, former governor Russell Alger of Michigan, former secretary of the treasury Walter Gresham of Indiana and Chauncey Depew, the president of the New York Central Railroad.

As early as May 1887, the *Los Angeles Times* reported on Allison's availability as "Republican Presidential Timber."[336] The March 17, 1888 edition of *Harper's Weekly* dedicated its entire front page to a portrait of the senator.[337] The boom was on for Allison, but what the Republican Party wanted and what it got were two different things.

The 1888 Republican National Convention voting progressed through eight ballots before settling on a nominee. John Sherman dominated the voting on the first six ballots but could not reach the prize. Allison did not receive the level of support in the convention that Sherman, Alger, Greshman or Harrison received, and dropped out after the seventh ballot.[338] As more of the nineteen contestants progressively dropped after ballot votes, a group of state delegates, including those from Iowa, Illinois, Wisconsin, Pennsylvania, New York and Massachusetts, met to decide on a candidate. U.S. senator George Hoar of Massachusetts stated in his autobiography that only one state delegate was missing from that meeting, and the group agreed that William Boyd Allison would be the next nominee. The missing delegate, New York's Chauncey Depew, the president

Harper's Weekly, March 17, 1888, with presidential-aspirant senator Allison on the cover. *Author's collection.*

of the New York Central Railroad and one of the contestants who recently dropped off the ballot, did not agree with his fellow New York delegates or those of the other states who agreed to nominate Allison. Depew threw his support to Benjamin Harrison, whose star continued to rise until finally, on the eighth ballot, Senator Harrison of Indiana won the requisite votes to become the Republican nominee for president. Senator Hoar wrote of Allison in his autobiography in 1903: "I think no other person ever came so near the presidency of the United States and missed it."[339]

Republican Benjamin Harrison defeated Democratic incumbent president Grover Cleveland to become the twenty-third president of the United States. It was Harrison's desire to have balance between the East and West in his cabinet. He intended to do that by making James Blaine of Maine his secretary of state and Allison his secretary of the treasury.

Harrison first offered Allison the Treasury Department around December 1, 1888. Harrison left the meeting under the impression that Allison would take the secretaryship. After receiving the acceptance of Blaine to be secretary of state, Harrison heard rumors that Allison was declining the treasury. The president-elect summoned Blaine and Allison to his home in Indianapolis on January 27, 1889, to settle the matter. On January 28, 1889, the *New York Times*'s headlines assured the nation, "Blaine and Allison Safe: Both Will Be Members of Harrison's Cabinet."[340]

On February 1, 1889, the *Washington Evening Star* reported that, for the second time—and once and for all—Senator Allison had declined Harrison's offer to become secretary of the treasury. Allison was keenly aware that if he joined the cabinet, his future prospects of becoming president would be greatly diminished.[341] Even though it caused great embarrassment to Harrison, who thought he could compel the senator to ultimately serve in his cabinet, Allison took the advice of his Republican friends in Congress and back home in Iowa and remained in the Senate. Just like President Garfield before him, President Harrison nominated William Windom of Minnesota to be his secretary of the treasury.

Allison's next—and, until now, what was believed to be his last opportunity—to ascend to the presidency came in 1896 in St. Louis, Missouri. Allison was one of six candidates vying for the nomination. Former Ohio governor Major William McKinley won the nomination on the first ballot.[342] McKinley would go on to beat Democrat William Jennings Bryan to become the twenty-fifth president of the United States.

McKinley, like Harrison and Garfield before him, wanted the calm and cool experience of Senator Allison in his cabinet. First, McKinley

The Senator Allison cigar, advertised and sold nationally by D.C. Glasser of Dubuque as "The Best 10-Cent Cigar in America," 1895. *Author's collection.*

offered Allison the position of secretary of state. Allison declined, making it known he wished to stay in the Senate. That secretaryship went to John Sherman.[343] McKinley then offered Allison the position of secretary of the treasury. Allison turned this offer down, too, and remained in the Senate.[344] Allison recognized the chairmanship of the critical Senate Appropriation Committee gave him the power to fund or defund any current or future legislative initiatives, making him one of the most powerful men in America.

On Wednesday, September 27, 1899, Senator Allison and Congressman D.B. Henderson, namesakes of Dubuque's Allison-Henderson Park, along with Captain John F. Merry, the assistant general passenger agent for the Illinois Central Railroad for Dubuque and East Dubuque, Illinois, met with

An 1896 presidential campaign ribbon with a portrait from the Allison Iowa Club. *Author's collection.*

Stuyvesant Fish, the president of the railroad, to discuss offering the use of the ICRR to help induce President McKinley to pay a visit to Dubuque during a planned trip to Omaha, Sioux City, Chicago and Milwaukee in mid-October. President McKinley accepted the railroad's offer, and plans were made for a presidential stop in Dubuque on October 16, 1899.[345]

This first visit to Dubuque of a sitting U.S. president was designed by Senator Allison and Representative Henderson to be a bipartisan affair. President Fish of the ICRR worked with his divisional superintendents to coordinate the transport of the president from Sioux City to Chicago, including his stops throughout Iowa. Division Superintendent E.H. Harriman, the New York railroad mogul, was the superintendent of the Dubuque district. President McKinley told Harriman during his thirty-five-minute stop in Dubuque, "I want to thank you for the splendid run you gave us last night, and I want to say that it is the first time since we left Washington that we have been on time."[346]

ICRR Engine No. 926, known as Old Reliable, pulled the president's and dignitaries' Pullman coaches from Waterloo, Iowa, to Dubuque, with special care given by engineer Harry Camp of Waterloo. Captain Merry was familiar with Camp's Ohio military service during the Civil War, so upon the return of the president to the train from Dubuque's Washington Park, Captain Merry took the opportunity to escort Camp, still in his dirty work overalls, into the president's private coach to introduce them. Mr. Camp reminded the president that they had been fellow soldiers together when McKinley's Twenty-Third Ohio Infantry drilled at Camp Chase in Columbus with Harry Camp's Twenty-Fourth Ohio Infantry at the start of the war. McKinley, always excited to meet a fellow comrade from the past, insisted on introducing Camp to Mrs. McKinley.[347]

Captain Merry had his own special moment with the president. Merry, along with Senator Allison and others, joined the president in Sioux City to escort the party across the state and into Dubuque. Arriving at a packed church in Sioux City on Sunday morning, Captain Merry was seated next to the president by the usher. Upon rising to give praise to the Lord from the hymn book, the president, seeing that Merry did not have a book, leaned into Merry and shared his hymnal as they offered their voices to the heavens. When Senator Allison formally introduced Merry to the president, Merry proclaimed with a sense of pride, "Why, this is the gentleman with whom I sang in the church!" The off-beat introduction brought joy to the president, as he continued to reference it throughout the day.[348] The historic Captain Merry Mansion, built in 1866, still stands today in East Dubuque, Illinois, and is currently an Airbnb.

Thirty-six days after President McKinley's visit to Dubuque, Vice President Garret Hobart passed away from heart disease. McKinley decided to wait until the election of 1900 to replace the vice president. The president's first and only choice to be his vice-presidential running mate was the senior senator from Iowa.

In March 1900, McKinley started to impress on Allison his desire to have him as his running mate. Allison, like Theodore Roosevelt, made it known that he was not interested in the vice presidency and would decline if nominated. Roosevelt, the former governor of New York and celebrated Rough Rider, was on a meteoric rise in popularity throughout America. But Roosevelt did not always toe the Republican Party line. Senator Mark Hanna of Ohio, a friend and chief advisor to the president, and President McKinley preferred their fellow Ohioan by birth William Boyd Allison.[349] Senator Nathan B. Scott of West Virginia verified what many had suspected at the time of Allison's death: President McKinley wanted only one person to be his running mate—Senator Allison.[350]

In a correspondence from Washington, the *New York Times* reported that individuals close to the senator did not think he would agree to be McKinley's running mate, observing, "Mr. Allison has been ambitious to be president and has felt himself to be close to the nomination on at least one occasion, but that has passed, and all his friends know that there is no position other than the one he now holds that has any attraction for him…his ambition now is to have a record of the longest continuous service in the Senate."[351]

On June 10, 1900, Charles Dawes, McKinley's Illinois campaign manager, wrote in his daily journal that he stopped at the executive mansion to visit the president and found Senators Allison and Hanna in conversation with the chief executive. Dawe's noted, "Allison persists that he will not accept the nomination for the vice presidency."[352]

It was generally believed going into the 1900 Republican National Convention in Philadelphia, held from June 19 to 21, that if Senator Allison would publicly indicate that he would accept the nomination, it would be his, regardless of Roosevelt. However, the father of the Senate did not acquiesce, so the rush was on for Roosevelt.[353]

Theodore Roosevelt received and accepted the nomination from the convention to be McKinley's running mate. President McKinley once again defeated Democrat William Jennings Bryan in the general election for a second term. Six months into his second term, on September 6, 1901, President McKinley was shot by an assassin in Buffalo, New York. The fallen commander-in-chief died on September 14, 1901. Vice President Theodore Roosevelt immediately became the twenty-sixth president of the United States.

The events of September 6–14, 1901, gave us the accidental presidency of Theodore Roosevelt. If Allison had chosen differently and accepted President McKinley's offer to be his vice presidential running mate, William Boyd Allison would have realized his dream of becoming president of the United States through the deranged actions of an assassin.

America's Best (And Most Valuable Public Man)

With the ascension of President Roosevelt, the elder Allison was content with providing sage advice to the young president. Allison spent the last eight years of his legislative career working on issues related to the railroads, currency, trade, tariffs and providing a buffer between the more cautious and methodical Congress and the brasher occupant of the executive mansion. Former president Roosevelt alluded to the respect and affection he had for the old-timer in a 1915 letter when he professed, "I was deeply attached to Senator Allison."[354]

"The Beloved Nestor of Republicanism," a 1902 Allison reelection broadside. *Author's collection.*

Allison also focused his last eight years on Iowa politics and his legacy. Allison was reelected to a sixth term in 1902 and was on track for the Iowa legislature to ratify a seventh term in Congress when the light at the dusk of Allison's life slipped into the shadow of death. On August 4, 1908, the sage of Dubuque passed away at his home at 1134 Locust Street in Dubuque, surrounded by his longtime household manager, Mrs. Brayton; Allison's close, personal Dubuque friend John McDonald; and his attending physician, Dr. John T. Hancock. The father of the Senate was dead, 191 days shy of his eightieth birthday.[355]

Telegrams came into Allison's private secretary, Lee McNeely, in Dubuque, expressing shock and sorrow at the passing of the beloved Nestor of the Senate. President Roosevelt sent a tribute from his home in Oyster Bay, New York. Vice President Fairbanks and Speaker Cannon arranged a large congressional delegation to attend the funeral in Dubuque, including the vice president. American poet and Allison's friend of forty-two years John A. Joyce, upon hearing of the death of the American statesmen, wrote a public tribute to the man many in the nation had come to count on, respect and admire.

WILLIAM BOYD ALLISON

A legislator of renown
Well known in every clime and town,
Has passed from this bright, vernal sod
To realms of glory with his God.

A man of pure and honest mind
And ever gracious, calm and kind,
Working in lane and field and wood
For all his human brotherhood.

His heart and hand were ever near
To help a comrade through all fear,
And when he could not praise your way
He did not have a word to say.

Peace to his ashes, long shall he
Inspire the noble and the free
O'er every mount and every sea
To stand and fight for liberty!

—*John A. Joyce, August 4, 1908, Washington, D.C.*[356]

William Boyd Allison was buried in Linwood Cemetery in Dubuque.

One must put into perspective the many facets of Allison's life's work to fully understand or appreciate the unwavering dedication and service of

William Boyd Allison to the citizens of Iowa and the people of the United States and his impact on history. Allison was by no means perfect, especially by today's standards. His imprudent role in early support for the creation of the Native boarding school system cannot be ignored.

At the time of his death in 1908, Allison was the longest-serving U.S. senator in history, the longest-serving congressman in congressional history and the longest-serving chair of a Senate committee, a record he still holds today.[357]

For the last decade or two of his political life, he was chairman of the powerful Senate Appropriation Committee, the second-ranking member on the Senate Finance Committee, the chairman of the Senate Republican Caucus and chairman of the Republican Steering Committee, making Senator Allison one of the most powerful men in American politics. No legislation could pass, no project could be initiated and no war could be funded without the consent of the senior senator from Iowa.[358]

Having played a role in all the major events that played out during the administrations of Presidents Lincoln, Johnson, Grant, Hayes, Garfield, Arthur, Cleveland (both nonconsecutive terms), Harrison, McKinley and Theodore Roosevelt, Allison is American history. From antislavery radicalism and Civil War to Constitutional amendments providing freedom; from the Whiskey Ring scandal to Crédit Mobilier; from southern Reconstruction to the Black Hills, Custer's folly and Native policy; from bimetallism to the gold standard; from annual federal budgets to the tariff question; from the Spanish-American War and the war in the Philippines to the building of the Panama Canal; and from the assassinations of Presidents Lincoln, Garfield and McKinley, to the death of the longest-serving congressman in U.S. history, few have played a front-and-center role, garnered the genuine praise and respect of their peers, received the gratitude of the nation and earned the title of father of the Senate more than William Boyd Allison.

NOTES

Chapter 1

1. Hebert L. Moeller and Hugh C. Mueller, "Lincoln and Grant in Iowa," IA GenWeb Special Project, http://iagenweb.org/history/history/oibg/Lincoln_Grant.htm.
2. Ibid.
3. W.K. Ackerman, *History of the Illinois Central Railroad Company and Representative Employees* (Chicago: Railroad Historical Company, 1900), 33.
4. Charles L. Brown, "Abraham Lincoln and the Illinois Central Railroad, 1857–1860," *Journal of the Illinois State Historical Society* 36, no. 2 (June 1943): 121–63.
5. Letter from John G. Drennan, district attorney, Illinois Central Railroad Company, to Professor Frank I. Herriott, Iowa State Historical Society, September 15, 1908.
6. Law Practice of Abraham Lincoln, "The Law Practice of Abraham Lincoln—Second Edition," http://www.lawpracticeofabrahamlincoln.org/Search.aspx.
7. Harry E. Pratt, *The Personal Finances of Abraham Lincoln* (Springfield, IL: Abraham Lincoln Association, 1943), 52.
8. Brown, "Lincoln and the Illinois Central Railroad," 121–63.
9. Ackerman, *History of the Illinois Central Railroad Company*, 36.
10. Carlton J. Corliss, *Abraham Lincoln and the Illinois Central Railroad, Main Line of Mid-America* (Chicago: Illinois Central, 1950), 11.
11. Brown, "Lincoln and the Illinois Central Railroad," 121–63.
12. Corliss, *Lincoln and the Illinois Central Railroad*, 11–12.
13. Mr. Lincoln and Friends, "The Politicians: Jesse K. Dubois (1811–1876)," http://www.mrlincolnandfriends.org/the-politicians/jesse-dubois.
14. Ibid.
15. Corliss, *Lincoln and the Illinois Central Railroad*, 12–13.
16. Brown, "Lincoln and the Illinois Central Railroad," 121–63.

17. Corliss, *Lincoln and the Illinois Central Railroad*, 13.

18. Ibid., 9.

19. Ibid., 13.

20. Wikipedia, "Panic of 1857," https://en.wikipedia.org/wiki/Panic_of_1857#cite_note-9.

21. Corliss, *Lincoln and the Illinois Central Railroad*, 14.

22. Wikipedia, "George B. McClellan," https://en.wikipedia.org/wiki/George_B._McClellan.

23. Corliss, *Lincoln and the Illinois Central Railroad*, 14.

24. Brown, "Lincoln and the Illinois Central Railroad," 121–63.

25. Law Practice of Abraham Lincoln, "Second Edition."

26. Ibid.

27. "Personal," *Dubuque Express and Herald*, April 28, 1859, 3.

28. "On an Inspecting Tour," *Freeport Weekly Journal*, July 21, 1859, 3.

29. "Assessment of the Illinois Central Road," *Chicago Tribune*, July 20, 1859, 1.

30. Corliss, *Lincoln and the Illinois Central Railroad*, 15.

31. "Assessment," *Chicago Tribune*, 1.

32. Mr. Lincoln and Friends, "The Politicians: Ozias M. Hatch (1814–1893)," http://www.mrlincolnandfriends.org/the-politicians/ozias-hatch/; Mr. Lincoln and Friends, "The Lawyers: Stephen Trigg Logan," http://www.mrlincolnandfriends.org/the-lawyers/stephen-trigg-logan/; Mr. Lincoln and Friends, "Jesse K. Dubois."

33. Lincoln Log, "A Daily Chronology of the Life of Abraham Lincoln," http://www.thelincolnlog.org/Results.aspx?type=basicSearch&terms=july+1859&r=L1NlYXJjaC5hc3B4.

34. C.H. Mottier, *Biography of Roswell B. Mason* (Chicago: Western Society of Engineers, 1938), 19–24.

35. "Hot Weather," *Dubuque Daily Times*, July 21, 1859, 2.

36. "Inspecting Tour," *Freeport Weekly Journal*, 3.

37. "Local News," *Dubuque Herald*, July 19, 1859, 3; "Inspecting Tour," *Freeport Weekly Journal*, 3.

38. John Carl Parish, *George Wallace Jones* (Iowa City: State Historical Society of Iowa, 1912), 238–39.

39. James B. Morrow, "Senator Allison's Reminiscences of His Forty-Three Years in Congress," *Washington Post*, May 10, 1908, 10.

40. "Interesting Story on Early History of Iowa in Magazine," *Telegraph-Herald and Times-Journal*, November 20, 1927, 1.

41. Ibid.

42. Ibid.

43. Parish, *George Wallace Jones*, 23.

44. *The History of Dubuque County, Iowa* (Chicago: Western Historical Company, 1880), 626–29.

45. "Senator Douglas—Is He with the North or South?," *Davenport Daily Gazette*, December 2, 1858, 2.

46. Warren W. Duncan, "The People v. Duleith Bridge Co., June 16, 1926," Court Listener, https://www.courtlistener.com/opinion/3421461/the-peopel-v-dunleith-bridge-co/.

47. "Mason, Bishop and Company," in *Dubuque City Directory* (Dubuque, IA: Times Book and Job Rooms, 1859), 57.

48. W.A. Adams, *Dubuque City Directory* (Dubuque, IA: W.A. Adams Publishing, 1856), 29.

49. "Law Intelligence," *Chicago Tribune*, September 21, 1857, 1.

50. Brown, "Lincoln and the Illinois Central Railroad," 121–63.

51. "Assessment," *Chicago Tribune*, 1.

52. *History of Dubuque County*, 530–31.

53. "Assessment," *Chicago Tribune*, 1.

54. Lincoln Log, "Daily Chronology."

55. Corliss, *Lincoln and the Illinois Central Railroad*, 15.

56. Brown, "Lincoln and the Illinois Central Railroad," 121–63.

57. Mr. Lincoln and Friends, "Jesse K. Dubois"; Mr. Lincoln and Friends, "Ozias M. Hatch."

58. Parish, *George Wallace Jones*, 235–47; Morrow, "Allison's Reminiscences," 10.

59. Mottier, *Biography*, 35–36.

60. "Chicago Relief: Special Session of the Council," *Dubuque Daily Herald*, October 11, 1871, 4.

Chapter 2

61. Alfred Aloe, *Twelfth U.S. Infantry, 1798–1919; Its Story, by Its Men* (New York: U.S. Army, 1919), 16–21.

62. "Major Rathbone," *Dubuque Democratic Herald*, April 18, 1865, 1.

63. Guy V. Henry, *Military Record of Civilian Appointments in the United States Army*, vol. 1 (New York: D. Van Nostrand Publishing, 1873), 424–25.

64. "Young, Able-Bodied Men," *Dubuque Daily Times*, March 6, 1862, 1.

65. Information was produced through qualitative and quantitative analysis by this author of the six-volume set of *Roster and Records of Iowa Soldiers in the War of the Rebellion, Together with Historical Sketches of Volunteer Organziations 1861–1866*, published in Des Moines, Iowa, by the adjutant general by authority of the Iowa General Assembly in 1908, 1910 and 1911.

66. Ibid.

67. Ibid.

68. "Capt. Washington Recruiting," *Dubuque Herald*, August 31, 1861, 4.

69. Henry, *Military Record*, 487.

70. *Journal of the Military Service Institution of the United States*, vol. 41 (Governor's Island, NY: Military Service Institution, 1907), 379.

71. Thomas H. Fearney, *Union College Alumni in the Civil War 1861–1865* (Schenectady, NY: Union College, 1915), 20, 39, 40.

72. Wikipedia, "Taps," https://en.wikipedia.org/wiki/Taps.

73. *Journal of the Military Service*, 379–93.

74. Ibid., 380–81.

75. "Young, Able-Bodied Men," *Dubuque Daily Times*, 1.

76. Geni, "Rev. Samuel Newbury," www.geni.com/people/Rev-Samuel-Newbury/6000000003508051115.

77. Encyclopedia Dubuque, "ADAMS, Austin," http://www.encyclopediadubuque.org/index.php?title=ADAMS,_Austin.

78. *Journal of the Military Service*, 379–93.

79. Wikipedia, "James Jackson (Medal of Honor)," https://en.wikipedia.org/wiki/James_Jackson_(Medal_of_Honor). It should be noted that James Jackson is often associated with the Twelfth Iowa Volunteer Infantry, which was also organized in Dubuque. This error seems to have originated with the State Historical Society of Iowa and the Iowa Medal of Honor Heroes Project. Nowhere in the rolls of the Twelfth Iowa Infantry is there listed a James Jackson. There is a James Jackson listed with the Twelfth U.S. Infantry, who was born in New Jersey and mustered into service in Dubuque, Iowa. It should also be noted that where James Jackson is mentioned with the Twelfth Iowa Infantry, it is also mentioned that the Twelfth Iowa left Dubuque to join the Army of the Potomac in the east. The Twelfth Iowa Infantry was never a member of the Army of the Potomac; however, the Twelfth U.S. Infantry was.

80. *Profound Poignant: Union College Connections to the Civil War Era* (Schenectady, NY: Union College, 2015), 12–21, www.union.edu/civilwar. Simplot also wrote correspondence for the *Dubuque Herald/Dubuque Democratic Herald* in 1861–62.

81. "Regimental Recruiting Service," *Philadelphia Inquirer*, May 5, 1863, 3.

82. Henry, *Military Record*, 424–25.

83. "Regimental Recruiting Service," *Philadelphia Inquirer*, 3.

84. Henry, *Military Record*, 425.

85. Ancestry, "Jared Lewis Rathbone CR6," https://www.ancestry.com/family-tree/person/tree/46155836/person/24090652243/facts.

86. Iowa State University Library Digital Collection, "Mary Newbury Adams Letters, 1861–1889," https://digitalcollections.lib.iastate.edu/islandora/object/isu%3AAdamsFamilyPapers_274.

87. Fearney, *Union College Alumni*, 39.

88. Henry, *Military Record*, 425.

89. Samuel S. Newbury's body was brought back to Dubuque and buried in Linwood Cemetery, next to the bodies of his sister and father and mother. The official story of his death states he was shot while surrendering. His being shot versus being taken prisoner could have been due in part to the fact General Grant had halted the prisoner exchange program shortly before Newbury's death.

Chapter 3

90. Lens of History, "Special Order No. 41," https://thelensofhistory.com/archives/letters-documents/special-order-no-41-general-vandever-leave-signed-by-lincoln-1863/.

91. "Congressional," *Huntington Democrat*, February 12, 1863, 1.

92. "The News," *New York Herald*, October 19, 1861, 4.

93. "The Congressman Colonel," *Dubuque Herald*, June 7, 1862, 1.

94. House of Representatives, *Byington vs. Vandever*, misc. doc. no. 6, 37th Congress, 2d Session, Washington, D.C., Government Printing Office, 1861, 1–3.

95. "New York, 22d," *Bangor Daily Whig and Courier* (ME), January 23, 1863, 3.

96. It is the author's claim that William Vandever was never formally expelled, nor was his seat formally vacated by himself or by an adopted resolution of the House of Representatives, allowing him to serve out his term at odds with article I, section 6, of the U.S. Constitution.

97. Biographical Directory of the United States Congress, "VANDEVER, William (1817–1893)," https://bioguideretro.congress.gov/Home/MemberDetails?memIndex =V000031.

98. Douglas Firth Anderson, "William Vandever: Presbyterian, Congressman, General," in *Dutch Americans and War: United States and Abroad*, edited by Robert P. Swierenga, Nella Kennedy and Lisa Zylstra (Holland, MI: Van Raalte Press, 2014), 53–66.

99. "Professional Cards—Samuels & Vandever," *Miners Express*, August 3, 1853, 1; "Professional Cards—Samuels & Vandever," *Miners Express*, August 9, 1854, 1.

100. Oliver P. Shiras, "Judge Oliver P. Shiras in Review of Early History of Dubuque County and the Dubuque Bar Association," *Dubuque Daily Times-Journal*, November 8, 1914, 2.

101. "William M. Stone, William Vandever, George T. Carpenter," *Annals of Iowa* 1, no. 3 (October 1893): 235–40.

102. Shiras, "Review of Early History of Dubuque," 2.

103. "Border State Committee," *National Republican*, January 3, 1861, 2.

104. "Congressional Proceedings," *Dubuque Weekly Times*, January 31, 1861, 8.

105. "Congressional," *Washington Evening Star*, February 16, 1861, 2.

106. "Union Inauguration Ball," *National Republican*, February 25, 1861, 2.

107. "Iowa Volunteers," *Dubuque Daily Times*, April 23, 1861, 2.

108. Lens of History, "Letter from Rep. Vandever to Charles Aldrich," https:// thelensofhistory.com/archives/letters-documents/u-s-rep-william-vandever-to-charles-aldrich/.

109. "Occupation of Fairfax-Particulars," *Green Mountain Freeman*, July 18, 1861, 2; "Reports from Fairfax Court House," *Chicago Tribune*, July 18, 1861, 1; "War News," *Huntington Globe*, July 18, 1861, 2.

110. "Interesting Capture of a Mammoth Secession Flag," *Madison State Journal*, November 25, 1861, 2.

111. "Preservation of the Constitution," *Buchanan County Guardian*, August 6, 1861, 4.

112. "Camp Union," *Madison State Journal*, September 12, 1861, 2.

113. Biographical Directory of the United States Congress, "VANDEVER."

114. Frederick H. Dyer, *Compendium of the War of the Rebellion* (Des Moines, IA: Dyer Publishing Co., 1908), 1,168–169; "Report of the Commissioners," *Dubuque Weekly Times*, December 5, 1861, 6.

115. "The News," *New York Herald*, 4.

116. Ibid.

117. "Our Readers Will Doubtless Remember…," *Pomeroy* (OH) *Weekly Telegraph*, November 1, 1861, 2.

118. House of Representatives, *Byington vs. Vandever*, misc. doc. no. 6, 37th Congress, 2d Session, Washington, D.C., Government Printing Office, 1861, 1–3.

119. Ibid.

120. "Residence of All the Senators and Members," *Philadelphia Inquirer*, December 10, 1861, 1.

121. Vote View, "Vandever, William (1817–1893)," https://voteview.com/person/9607/william-vandever.

122. "Army Correspondence," *Dubuque Daily Times*, February 6, 1862, 2.

123. Dyer, *Compendium*, 1,168–169.

124. American Battlefield Trust, "Pea Ridge—Elkhorn Tavern," https://www.battlefields.org/learn/civil-war/battles/pea-ridge.

125. "A Marching Record," *Grant County Witness* (WI), June 5, 1862, 1.

126. "Washington Correspondence," *Burlington Hawkeye*, April 12, 1862, 1.

127. "Contested Election Case," *National Republican*, May 9, 1862, 1.

128. Ibid.

129. Ibid.

130. Vote View, "Vandever, William"; "May 9, 1862," in *Journal of the House of Representatives of the United States: Being the Second Session of the Thirty-Seventh Congress* (Washington, D.C.: Government Printing Office, 1862), 662–65.

131. Wikipedia, "William Vandever," https://en.wikipedia.org/wiki/William_Vandever.

132. "Congressman Colonel," *Dubuque Herald*, 1.

133. William E. Wilkie, *Dubuque on the Mississippi 1788–1988* (Dubuque, IA: Loras College Press, 1988), 223.

134. Harry Slichter, "Dubuque Editors and the Civil War," *Dubuque Telegraph-Herald*, February 4, 1966, 4.

135. "Arrest of the Editor of the Dubuque Herald," *New York Times*, August 15, 1862, 8.

136. Edward F. Mason, "Congressional Redistricting Since 1847," in *Iowa Official Register, Fiftieth Number, 1963–1964* (Des Moines: Iowa State Press, 1963), 381–85.

137. "The Nomination of D.A. Mahony," *Buchanan County Guardian*, August 26, 1862, 2.

138. "Congressional Nominees," *Cedar Falls Gazette*, August 22, 1862, 2.

139. "The News of Saturday," *Burlington Daily Hawk Eye Gazette*, September 1, 1862, 2.

140. Encyclopedia Dubuque, "MAHONY, Dennis," http://www.encyclopediadubuque.org/index.php?title=MAHONY,_Dennis.

141. "Recent and Still Pending," *Chicago Tribune*, January 24, 1863, 1; "New York, 22d," *Bangor Daily Whig and Courier* (ME), 3. The Congressmen included Senator James Henry Lane (R-KS) and Representatives Edwin Hanson Webster (U-MD), Robert Bruce Van Valkenburgh (R-NY), Francis William Kellogg (R-MI), William Vandever (R-IA), Charles John Biddle (D-PA), Philip B. Fouke (D-IL),

James Kerrigan (D-NY), James Hepburn Campbell (R-PA), Alexander S. Diven (R-NY), Richard Franchot (R-NY), James B. McKean (R-NY), Socrates N. Sherman (R-NY), Charles Van Wyck (R-NY), Gilman Marston (R-NH), William McKee Dunn (R-IN), John A. Gurley (R-OH), Edward McPherson (R-PA) and John P.C. Shanks (R-IN).

142. "Washington Correspondent," *Burlington Hawkeye*, December 18, 1862, 2.

143. Vote View, "37th Congress>House>Vote 380," https://voteview.com/rollcall/RH0370380.

144. "Washington News, 20th," *Daily Democrat and News*, January 22, 1863, 1.

145. Ibid.

146. Ibid.

147. Ibid.

148. "Thirty-Seventh Congress," *Lancaster Examiner and Herald*, January 28, 1863, 3.

149. "January 21, 1863," in *Journal of the House of Representatives of the United States: Being the Third Session of the Thirty-Seventh Congress* (Washington, D.C.: Government Printing Office, 1863), 214–220.

150. "490. The Iowa Election Case of Byington v. Vandever, in the Thirty-Seventh Congress," in *Hinds' Precedents of the House of Representatives of the United States* (Washington, D.C.: Government Printing Office, 1907), 596–99.

151. "Washington News," *Daily Democrat and News*, 1; "Colonel Vandever," *Dubuque Daily Times*, June 7, 1862, 2.

152. Lens of History, "Special Order No. 41."

153. "February 14, 1863," in *Journal of the House of Representatives of the United States: Being the Third Session of the Thirty-Seventh Congress* (Washington, D.C.: Government Printing Office, 1863), 401–2; "Iowa Contested Election," *Washington National Intelligencer*, February 19, 1863, 1.

154. "February 25, 1863," in *Journal of the House of Representatives of the United States: Being the Third Session of the Thirty-Seventh Congress* (Washington, D.C.: Government Printing Office, 1863), 480–84.

155. "Commerce Between East and West," *National Intelligencer*, March 5, 1863, 2.

156. "Death of General Vandever," *Californian*, July 25, 1893, 1.

157. Lens of History, "Special Order No. 41."

158. Biographical Directory of the U.S. Congress, "LANE, James Henry," https://bioguideretro.congress.gov/Home/MemberDetails?memIndex=L000061.

Chapter 4

159. Leland L. Sage, *William Boyd Allison: A Study in Practical Politics* (Iowa City: State Historical Society of Iowa, 1956), 61–85.

160. Wendell Phillips advertisement, *Dubuque Daily Herald*, February 10, 1867, 1. The president of the YMLA in 1865 and 1866 was Oliver P. Shiras, the Dubuque attorney who served as aide-de-camp to his cousin and fellow Dubuquer Brigadier General Francis J. Herron during the Civil War. Herron served under William Vandever in the Ninth Iowa Infantry at the start of the Civil War. Oliver Shiras

was the brother of future U.S. Supreme Court justice George Shiras Jr. George Shiras briefly practiced law in Dubuque from 1855 to 1858.

161. Wendell Phillips advertisement, *Dubuque Daily Herald*, 1.

162. "Fred. Douglass Is to Lecture in Dubuque," *Dubuque Daily Times*, April 15, 1866, 4.

163. Encyclopedia Dubuque, "ADAMS, Austin."

164. "Douglass," *Dubuque Daily Herald*, April 21,1866, 1.

165. "How Negroes Wrongs Pay," *Dubuque Daily Herald*, March 6, 1867, 2.

166. "Young Men's Literary Association," in *Dubuque City Directory 1865–66*, (Dubuque, IA: Dubuque Daily Hearld, 1865), 37.

167. Encyclopedia Dubuque, "WOOD, George," http://www.encyclopediadubuque.org/index.php?title=WOOD,_George.

168. Encyclopedia Dubuque, "*Dubuque Herald*," http://www.encyclopediadubuque.org/index.php?title=DUBUQUE_HERALD; Encyclopedia Dubuque, "*Dubuque Times*," http://www.encyclopediadubuque.org/index.php?title=DUBUQUE_TIMES.

169. "The President to Issue Nigger Proclamation," *Dubuque Daily Herald*, July 11, 1862, 1; "Impeachment Thrown Overboard," *Dubuque Daily Herald*, December 10, 1867, 2; "Manchester," *Dubuque Daily Herald*, January 31, 1867, 1.

170. "Douglass Is to Lecture," *Dubuque Daily Times*, 4.

171. "The Lecture," *Dubuque Daily Herald*, April 21, 1866, 4; Wikipedia, "William Vandever."

172. "Lecture," *Dubuque Daily Herald*, 4.

173. Ibid., 4.

174. Frederick Douglass advertisement, *Dubuque Daily Herald*, March 3, 1868, 1.

175. Wikipedia, "Self-Made Man," https://en.wikipedia.org/wiki/Self-Made_Men.

176. Frederick Douglass advertisement, *Dubuque Daily Herald*, 1; IAGenWeb, "A.T. Andreas Illustrated Historical Atlas of the State of Iowa," http://files.usgwarchives.net/ia/dubuque/history/dubuque.txt.

177. "Lecture," *Dubuque Daily Herald*, 4.

178. Cody Marrs, "Frederick Douglass and the Long Civil War," Cambridge University Press, http://www.cambridgeblog.org/2015/07/frederick-douglass-and-the-long-civil-war/.

179. Encyclopedia Dubuque, "ROOT, Samuel," http://www.encyclopediadubuque.org/index.php?title=ROOT,_Samuel.

180. John Stauffer, Zoe Trodd and Celeste-Marie Bernier, *Picturing Frederick Douglass: An Illustrated Biography of the Nineteenth Century's Most Photographed American* (New York City: W.W. Norton & Company, 2015), 54.

181. "Iowa Condensed Items, Samuel Root," *Pocahontas County Sun*, March 21, 1889, 1; Art Blart, "Marcus Aurelius Root," https://artblart.com/tag/marcus-aurelius-root/.

182. The images of Bishop Simpson and General Herron are in the author's collection.

183. The author visited the Gilder-Lehrman Institute and viewed the image on September 20, 2017.

184. Stauffer, Trodd and Bernier, *Picturing Frederick Douglass*, 54; Robert S. Levine and Samuel Otter, *Frederick Douglass and Herman Melville: Essays in Relation* (Chapel

Hill: University of North Carolina Press Books, 2008), 321–26; Gilder-Lehrman Institute of American History, "Douglass, Frederick (1818–1895) Half-Length Seated Carte De Visite Portrait of Frederick Douglass, With Cane," https://www.gilderlehrman.org/collections/66eef4af-6bf8-459e-92af-159481734600?back=/mweb/search%3Fneedle%3DGLC07752%2A%2526fields%3D_t301001010.

185. O.E. Root, *Root's Dubuque City Directory* (Dubuque, IA: Times Book and Jobs Room, 1867), 136; J.M. Wolfe, *Dubuque City Directory* (Dubuque, IA: J.M. Wolf Publisher, 1868), 174.

186. "The Movement of Fred," *Dubuque Daily Herald*, April 22, 1866, 4.

187. Stauffer, Trodd and Bernier, *Picturing Frederick Douglass*, iv.

188. Find-a-Grave, "Samuel Root," https://www.findagrave.com/memorial/7584185/samuel-root.

Chapter 5

189. Iowa Data Center, "Total Population for Iowa's Incorporated Places: 1850–2010," www.iowadatacenter.com.

190. "In Camp: The Nation's Pride from Far and Near," *Dubuque Hearld*, June 17, 1884, 3.

191. "The Bloodless Battle: The Elements at War with the Militia," *Dubuque Herald*, June 21, 1884, 3.

192. Captain William H. Powell, *Report of the Secretary of War; Being Part of the Message and Documents Communicated to the Two Houses of Congress* (Washington, D.C.: Government Printing Office, 1884), 269–76.

193. Logan, *Roster and Record*, 62–65.

194. "The Encampment: The Rain and Unfortunate Blow to Yesterday's Programme, the Competitive Drill to Take Place To-day," *Dubuque Herald*, June 19, 1884, 3.

195. "National Encampment at Dubuque, Iowa," *United States Army and Navy Journal and Gazette of the Regular and Volunteer Forces*, May 24, 1884, 886.

196. All Biographies, "Charles S. Bentley," http://www.all-biographies.com/soldiers/charles_s_bentley.htm.

197. "In Camp," *Dubuque Herald*, 3.

198. "The Encampment," *Dubuque Herald*, 3.

199. Ibid., 1.

200. "Grant County in the Civil War," in *History of Grant County Wisconsin* (Chicago: Western Historical Company, 1881), 593–638.

201. Wikipedia, "John Gibbon," https://en.wikipedia.org/wiki/John_Gibbon.

202. "In Camp," *Dubuque Herald*, 3.

203. Powell, *Report of the Secretary of War*, 269–76.

204. Ibid.

205. Ibid.

206. Ibid.

207. Ibid.

208. "Incidents," *Dubuque Times*, June 19, 1884, 6.
209. Powell, *Report of the Secretary of War*, 269–76.
210. "Incidents," *Dubuque Times*, 6.
211. "General Notes," *Dubuque Times*, June 21, 1884, 7.
212. "The Gala Day," *Dubuque Times*, June 21, 1884, 6.
213. "The Gambling Nuisance," *Dubuque Daily Times*, June 19, 1884, 6.
214. Powell, *Report of the Secretary of War*, 269–76; "Incidents," *Dubuque Times*, 6.
215. "The Roller Rinks," *Dubuque Times*, June 19, 1884, 7.
216. Ibid., 7.
217. "Police Pointers," *Dubuque Times*, June 22, 1884, 7.
218. "General Notes," *Dubuque Times*, 7.
219. Ibid., 6.
220. Powell, *Report of the Secretary of War*, 269–76.
221. Ibid.
222. Ebay, "1884 CIVIL WAR TROPHY BUSCH ZOUAVES 8ᵀᴴ MISSOURI INFANTRY PRESENTATION PITCHER," purchased by author on April 25, 2017, from davitcio, http://www.ebay.com.
223. "The Encampment: The Reason the Tredways Did Not Receive the First Prize," *Dubuque Herald*, June 24, 1884, 3.
224. "Knight, Alonzo R.," in *Dubuque City Directory 1884–85* (Chicago: R.L Polk & Co., 1884), 232.
225. "Camp Notes," *Dubuque Times*, June 18, 1884, 6.
226. "Dickson's Sketch Club," *Dubuque Times*, June 20, 1884, 6.

Chapter 6

227. Andrew Carnegie, *Autobiography of Andrew Carnegie* (Boston: Riverside Press Cambridge, 1920), 123–25.
228. "William Boyd Allison," *Magazine of Western History* 6, no. 1 (May 1887): 65.
229. "William Boyd Allison," *Dubuque Telegraph-Herald and Times Journal*, March 3, 1929, 22.
230. Ibid.
231. "William Boyd Allison," *Magazine of Western History*, 67.
232. Shiras, "Review of Early History of Dubuque," 2.
233. Weston A. Goodspeed and Kenneth C. Goodspeed, *History of Dubuque County, Iowa* (Chicago: Goodspeed Historical Association, 1911), 761.
234. Sage, *William Boyd Allison*, 37.
235. "William Boyd Allison," *Dubuque Telegraph-Herald and Times Journal*, 22.
236. Sage, *William Boyd Allison*, 34–35.
237. Morrow, "Allison's Reminiscences," 10.
238. Ibid.
239. Sage, *William Boyd Allison*, 4.
240. "Death Releases 'Dave' Henderson," *Chicago Daily Tribune*, February 26, 1906, 5.
241. Mason, "Congressional Redistricting," 381–85.

242. Wilkie, *Dubuque on the Mississippi*, 223.

243. "Arrest of the Editor," *New York Times*, 8; Encyclopedia Dubuque, "MAHONY, Dennis."

244. "The Arrest of Mahony," *Burlington Daily Hawk Eye Gazette*, August 18, 1862, 2.

245. "The Story of the Herald," *Dubuque Semi-Centennial Herald*, May 9, 1886, 1.

246. "Ousted," *Burlington Daily Hawk Eye Gazette*, November 29, 1862, 2.

247. "Story of the Herald," *Dubuque Semi-Centennial Herald*, 1.

248. "John Taylor Adams, Noted Republican Party Leader, Dies at Home in Dubuque," *Dubuque Telegraph-Herald*, October 29, 1939, 1. John Taylor Adams served twelve years on the Republican National Committee and served as the RNC chairman from 1921 to 1924. Taylor helped direct the presidential campaigns for Warren G. Harding and Calvin Coolidge and was a friend of fellow eastern Iowan Herbert Hoover. Taylor and his wife were close personal friends of President Calvin Coolidge and Mrs. Coolidge.

249. "Abolition Republican Nomination," *Dubuque Daily Herald*, August 8, 1862, 1.

250. "Democratic Congressional Convention," *New Oregon Plain Dealer*, August 29, 1862, 2.

251. "Nomination," *Buchanan County Guardian*, 2.

252. "The Wrong Principle—Stilson Hutchins," *Burlington Daily Hawk Eye Gazette*, October 2, 1862, 3.

253. "William Boyd Allison," *Magazine of Western History*, 68.

254. Ibid.

255. Frank G. Carpenter, "William B. Allison: A Visit to the Iowa Statesman and a Pleasant Chat with Him," *Los Angeles Times*, June 23, 1895, 17.

256. Wikipedia, "List of Members of the United States Congress by Longevity of Service," https://en.wikipedia.org/wiki/List_of_members_of_the_United_States_Congress_by_longevity_of_service.

257. "William Boyd Allison," *Magazine of Western History*, 69.

258. "Ruler of the Senate: Allison, of Iowa, Benevolent but Firm Dictator," *Washington Post*, February 26, 1905, E3.

259. Congressional Medal of Honor Society, "Medal of Honor History & Timeline," https://www.cmohs.org/medal/timeline.

260. Phil Edwards, "The Horrific Spike in Whiskey Prices During the Civil War, in One Chart," Vox, https://www.vox.com/2015/8/7/9111123/whiskey-civil-war-chart#:~:text=And%20in%201862%2C%20Congress%20set,year%20the%20Civil%20War%20ended.

261. Ainsworth R. Spofford, *American Almanac and Treasury of Facts, Statistical, Financial, and Political, for the Year 1888* (New York: American News Company, 1888), 102.

262. "The Dubuque Whiskey Fraud," *Chicago Tribune*, February 22, 1866, 2.

263. Ibid.

264. "The Distillery Fraud: The Suppressed Documents," *Dubuque Daily Herald*, October 6, 1866, 2.

265. Ibid.

266. "The Last Manifesto of the Enemy: A Complete Answer to the Lying Charges, Mr. Allison Vindicated," *Dubuque Daily Times*, October 27, 1868, 5.

267. "The Distillery Fraud: Wm. B. Allison Badly Mixed Up in It," *Dubuque Daily Herald*, October 6, 1866, 1.

268. "Ex. Doc. No. 21, Letter of the Secretary of the Treasury," in *U.S. Senate, 39th Congress, 1st Session* (Washington, D.C.: Government Print Office, 1866), 10.

269. Ibid., 2.

270. Wikipedia, "Whiskey Ring," https://en.wikipedia.org/wiki/Whiskey_Ring.

271. John A. Joyce, *Checkered Life* (Chicago: S.P. Rounds Jr., 1883), 134–49.

272. "Col. Joyce Here to See Old Friends," *Dubuque Telegraph-Herald*, August 31, 1904, 5.

273. "Letters from *Sunday Post-Dispatch* Readers Concerning the Wilcox-Joyce Controversy," *St. Louis Post-Dispatch*, August 13, 1899, 22.

274. "Col. John A. Joyce," *Louisville Courier-Journal*, November 23, 1887, 5.

275. "Upon a Compromise," *Times-Picayune*, November 4, 1888, 4.

276. "Ella Wheeler Wilcox and Col. John A. Joyce," *El Paso Herald*, August 30, 1902, 2.

277. "Vice President and Director," *Dubuque Daily Times*, August 21, 1867, 4.

278. Robert W. Jackson, "Extant Approach Spans of the Dunleith and Dubuque Bridge," *Journal of the Society for Industrial Archeology* 31, no. 1 (2005): 5.

279. Carnegie, *Autobiography*, 123–25.

280. Ibid.

281. Mottier, *Biography*, 35–36.

282. Wikipedia, "Oakes Ames," https://en.wikipedia.org/wiki/Oakes_Ames.

283. PBS, "The Transcontinental Railroad: Oakes Ames," https://www.pbs.org/wgbh/americanexperience/features/tcrr-ames/.

284. Wikipedia, "Crédit Mobilier scandal," https://en.wikipedia.org/wiki/Cr%C3%A9dit_Mobilier_scandal.

285. Abraham Lincoln Papers at the Library of Congress, "From William T. Otto to Abraham Lincoln, September 14, 1864," https://www.loc.gov/item/mal3630700/.

286. O.E. Root, "Railroads and Coal Company," in *Root's Dubuque City Directory*, 170.

287. "Crédit Mobilier: Interesting Testimony," *Dubuque Daily Times*, January 25, 1873, 2.

288. "Testimony of Oakes Ames Relative to Crédit Mobilier," *Dubuque Daily Times*, January 8, 1873, 1.

289. "The Crédit Mobilier Investigation—Interesting Cross Examination—Mr. Allison's Denial," *Dubuque Daily Times*, January 8, 1873, 1.

290. "Interesting Testimony," *Dubuque Daily Times*, 2.

291. Biographical Directory of the United States Congress, "AMES, Oakes; 1804–1873," https://bioguide.congress.gov/search/bio/A000175l.

292. GovTrack, "Sen. William Allison," https://www.govtrack.us/congress/members/william_allison/400815.

293. Sage, *William Boyd Allison*, 129–30.

294. Bradley R. Rice, "Commission Form of City Government," Texas State Historical Association, https://www.tshaonline.org/handbook/entries/commission-form-of-city-government.

295. Biographical Directory of the United States Congress, "ALLISON, William Boyd, 1873–1908," https://bioguideretro.congress.gov/Home/MemberDetails ?memIndex=A000160.

296. William B. Allison, *Report of the Commission Appointed to Treat with the Sioux Indians for the Relinquishment of the Black Hills* (Washington, D.C.: Government Printing Office, 1875), 4–7.

297. "Nebraska: Ground for the Big Talk Hard to Agree Upon," *Dubuque Daily Times*, September 25, 1875, 1.

298. Allison, *Report of the Commission*, 7–9.

299. Ibid.

300. Ibid., 17.

301. Ibid., 7–9.

302. Ibid., 18.

303. Ibid., 18.

304. Ibid., 18.

305. John D. McDermott, "The Military Problem and the Black Hills, 1874–1875," *South Dakota History* 31, nos. 3 and 4 (Fall/Winter 2001): 188–210.

306. "From Inspector Vandever to Commissioner Smith, May 22, 1876," Papers of William Vandever, University of Dubuque, Charles M. Meyers Library Archives.

307. "From Inspector Vandever to Secretary Chandler, May 22, 1876," Papers of William Vandever, University of Dubuque, Charles M. Meyers Library Archives.

308. "The Indian War," *Dubuque Daily Times*, July 9, 1876, 4.

309. Ibid.

310. Ibid.

311. William Vandever, "The Sioux War: The Whole Indian Question Succinctly Reviewed by Gen. Vandever," *Dubuque Daily Times*, August 6, 1876, 4.

312. Richmond L. Clow, "The Sioux Nation and Indian Territory: The Attempted Removal of 1876," *South Dakota History* 6, no. 4 (Fall 1976): 456–73.

313. Ibid.

314. "Going Among the Indians," *Dubuque Daily Herald*, August 26, 1876, 4.

315. Clow, "Sioux Nation and Indian Territory," 456–73.

316. Encyclopedia Dubuque, "COOLEY, D.N.," https://www.encyclopediadubuque. org/index.php/COOLEY,_D._N.

317. Wikipedia, "Johnson Chestnut Whittaker," https://en.wikipedia.org/wiki/ Johnson_Chesnut_Whittaker.

318. "WASHINGTON: Why the Colored Boys Were Not Admitted at West Point," *New York Times*, June 11, 1870, 5.

319. "Colored Cadets at West Point," *New York Times*, April 27, 1880, 1.

320. Ibid.

321. "The Colored Cadet Debate," *New York Times*, April 30, 1880, 5.

322. "Race Equality at West Point," *New York Times*, May 1, 1880, 1.

323. "Adding to the Retired List," *New York Times*, May 21, 1880, 5.

324. United States Senate, "Shaving and Saving: The Story of Bishop Sims," https://www.senate.gov/artandhistory/senate-stories/Shaving-and-Saving-the-Story-of-Bishop-Sims.htm.

325. "To William Boyd Allison," in *Booker T. Washington Papers*, vol. 4 (Champaign: University of Illinois Press, 1975), 159.

326. University of Chicago Library, "Guide to the Allison Davis Papers 1932–1984," https://www.lib.uchicago.edu/e/scrc/findingaids/view.php?eadid=ICU.SPCL.DAVISA&q=Anthropologists.

327. Wikipedia, "Bland-Allison Act," https://en.wikipedia.org/wiki/Bland%E2%80%93Allison_Act.

328. "Allison and Wilson," *Dubuque Daily Times*, March 12, 1880, 2.

329. "The Cabinet," *Dubuque Daily Times*, March 6, 1881, 3.

330. Ibid.

331. "President Garfield's Cabinet," *Washington Evening Star*, March 5, 1881, 1.

332. "Senator Allison's Excuse," *Dubuque Daily Times*, March 18, 1881, 2.

333. "A Senator's Wife Tries to Drown Herself," *Washington Post*, September 8, 1881, 2.

334. "BY HER OWN HAND: The Wife of United States Senator Allison…," *Chicago Daily Tribune*, August 14, 1883, 2.

335. William B. Allison was born on March 2, 1829. Mary Nealley was born on January 17, 1849.

336. Alfred Sorenson, "Senator Allison: A Correspondent Interviews Senator Madnerson," *Los Angeles Times*, May 25, 1887, 9.

337. "Senator William B. Allison of Iowa," *Harper's Weekly*, March 17, 1888, 1.

338. Wikipedia, "1888 Republican National Convention," https://en.wikipedia.org/wiki/1888_Republican_National_Convention.

339. George F. Hoar, *Autobiography of Seventy Years* (New York: Charles Scribner's Sons, 1903), 409–13.

340. "Blaine and Allison Safe," *New York Times*, January 28, 1889, 1.

341. "Senator Allison Declines," *Washington Evening Star*, February 1, 1889, 1.

342. Wikipedia, "1896 Republican National Convention," https://en.wikipedia.org/wiki/1896_Republican_National_Convention.

343. "Allison Declines," *Washington Evening Star*, 10.

344. "Political Notes," *Washington National Tribune*, January 14, 1897, 8.

345. "McKinley May Come Here," *Dubuque Daily Herald*, September 30, 1899, 8.

346. "President in Dubuque: What the President Said," *Dubuque Daily Herald*, October 17, 1899, 8.

347. "Comrades Meet," *Dubuque Daily Times*, October 17, 1899, 4.

348. "Merry Honored," *Dubuque Daily Times*, October 17, 1899. 2.

349. "Both Want a Man for Second Place," *Janesville Daily Gazette*, June 8, 1900, 1.

350. "Was Choice of McKinley: Nestor of Senate Wanted as a Running Mate," *Dubuque Telegraph-Herald*, August 6, 1908, 1 and 7.

351. "Senator Allison's Ambition," *New York Times*, April 22, 1900, 1.

352. Charles G. Dawes, *A Journal of the McKinley Years* (Chicago: Lakeside Press, 1950), 230–31.

353. "A Rush to Roosevelt," *Baltimore Sun*, June 18, 1900, 2.

354. "Letter from Theodore Roosevelt to E.R. Harlan," Theodore Roosevelt Digital Library, Dickinson State University, https://www.theodorerooseveltcenter.org/Research/Digital-Library/Record?libID=o212141.

355. "Death Came Suddenly: Brough Home to Die, Beginning of the End," *Chicago Daily Tribune*, August 5, 1908, 2.

356. John A. Joyce, "William Boyd Allison," *Dubuque Times-Journal*, August 9, 1908, 6.

357. United States Senate, "Facts & Milestones: Record Holders," https://www.senate.gov/artandhistory/history/common/briefing/Facts_Figures.htm.

358. "Allison's Senate Record the Longest in History," *Alta Advertiser*, August 14, 1908, 7.

INDEX

U

Union Pacific Railroad 88, 99, 100

V

Vandever, William 45, 46, 47, 48, 49,
        50, 51, 52, 53, 54, 55, 56, 57,
        58, 59, 60, 61, 62, 66, 87, 89,
        105, 107, 109, 127, 128, 129

W

Washburne, Elihu 50, 54, 57, 58
Washington, Booker T. 112
Washington, Edward C. 39
Whiskey Ring 94, 96, 97, 122

Y

Yates, Richard 24

ABOUT THE AUTHOR

*J*ohn T. Pregler is an independent researcher, historian and author by night and an engineering and information solutions consultant by day.

John was born and raised in Dubuque, Iowa, where his family has resided since the 1840s. John has been studying local and regional history of national importance for as long as he can remember and started conducting research and collecting information and artifacts on a variety of topics starting in the late 1970s, when he learned his great-great-grandfather George Pregler and his brother John served in the Civil War from 1861 to 1865 in Iowa military units.

Two of John's favorite topics to study, lecture on and write about are the American Civil War and early American baseball. John is a member of the Sons of Union Veterans of the Civil War (SUVCW) and the Society for American Baseball Research (SABR).

John is the proprietor of the website www.thelensofhistory.com.

Visit us at
www.historypress.com